Programs and manifestoes on 20th-century architecture

Programs and manifestoes

Translated by Michael Bullock

Edited by Ulrich Conrads

on 20th-century architecture

The MIT Press, Cambridge, Massachusetts

First English language edition, 1970
First MIT Press paperback edition, 1975

Third printing, 1977

Fourth printing, 1980

ISBN 0 262 03039 X (hardcover)
ISBN 0 262 53030 9 (paperback)
Library of Congress Catalog No. 71-143178

Publishers' note:
Michael Bullock has translated all the extracts in this book with the
exception of those commencing on pages 25, 49, 59, 69, 95, 117, 124, 146,
154, 163, 169, 179. These are reprinted from existing texts in English, either
original or in translation, by kind permission of the publishers concerned.
(All sources are listed, commencing on page 187.) Where extracts have been
taken from American works, these have been made to conform to English
usage in common with the rest of this book.

Printed in the United States of America

WORK SONG   FRANK LLOYD WRIGHT

I'LL LIVE
AS I'LL WORK
AS I AM!
NO WORK IN FASHION FOR SHAM
NOR TO FAVOUR FORSWORN
WEAR MASK CREST OR THORN
MY WORK AS BEFITTETH A MAN
MY WORK
WORK THAT BEFITTETH THE MAN

I'LL WORK
AS I'LL THINK
AS I AM!
NO THOUGHT OF FASHION OR SHAM
NOR FOR FORTUNE THE JADE
SERVE VILE GODS-OF-TRADE
MY THOUGHT AS BESEEMETH A MAN
MY THOUGHT
THOUGHT THAT BESEEMETH THE MAN

I'LL THINK
AS I'LL ACT
AS I AM!
NO DEED IN FASHION FOR SHAM
NOR FOR FAME EER MAN MADE
SHEATH THE NAKED WHITE BLADE
MY ACT AS BECOMETH A MAN
MY ACT
ACTS THAT BECOMETH THE MAN

I'LL ACT
AS I'LL DIE
AS I AM!
NO SLAVE OF FASHION OR SHAM
OF MY FREEDOM PROUD
HERS TO SHRIVE GUARD OR SHROUD
MY LIFE AS BETIDETH THE MAN
MY LIFE
AYE! WHATEVER BETIDETH THE MAN

DECLARATION OF INDEPENDENCE. T-SQUARE AND TRIANGLE VERSES. OAK PARK WORKSHOP 1896

Contents

Foreword

The wish to see the many programmatic statements on architecture assembled in a form in which they could be easily studied was aroused by the most apparently eccentric architectural manifesto of recent years. Anyone who in 1958 saw Hundertwasser's *Mould Manifesto against rationalism in architecture* may perhaps have reacted like the editor of this present work: he was less surprised by the protest as such – even at this time it was impossible to close one's ears to the voices raised against functional architecture – than staggered by the crass subjectivity with which the buildings of two generations were condemned to wholesale destruction and dismissed as uninhabitable. There has really been no lack of critical and revolutionary actions and statements during this century. But never before had building been so recklessly handed over to the anarchical caprice of the individual; never before had the demand been so loudly voiced that buildings should be left to the mercy of the 'creative' forces of the natural processes of dilapidation. It is true that the utterances of the Lettrists and the later Situationists, which from 1954 on are to be found in the most varied – chiefly literary – periodicals, also cast fundamental doubt on rational building and functional planning; but they are far from offering as a solution to urgent problems uncommitted action or uncommitted *laisser-faire*. On the contrary, they demand consistent regard for locality and specific situation. The 'new games' for which they call do not by any means imply that construction and town planning should be carried out without reference to the surroundings, but would rather necessitate a renewed use of the creative imagination based on precise observation of the complex interconnected structures of the city. And when – to take another example – Marinetti, forty years before, in the appendices to the 'gospel' of Sant'Elia in 1914, attacked the 'whole of modern architecture' and declared that dynamic building could not exist without slanting or elliptical lines, he too was not aiming either at unconstraint or anarchy in building, but at exactly the opposite: at 'the architecture of calculation'. The reader will have no difficulty in discovering other similarly provocative connexions or contradictions in the manifestoes, programmes, and programmatic essays gathered together in this volume, any one of which might have provided the incentive for this collection.

The choice – and selection has been at work here – is consciously limited to texts dating from this century. Two further determining factors governed the selection: only those texts were chosen which on the one hand represent the starting point, or a definite stage, of a particular development in architecture, and on the other exercised a determining influence on architecture within the area of Central Europe. All the texts are arranged according to the year of their first publication. Within each year, however, this chronological order has been abandoned in favour of certain comparative confrontations. In the case of essays it was not always possible to avoid abbreviation; in each case there is a note to this effect. For permission to reprint the editor owes his explicit thanks to the authors and the publishers listed in the index of sources.

UC

1903 Henry van de Velde: Programme

The 'new departure of 1900' had in Henry van de Velde (b.1863 in Antwerp, d.1957 in Zürich) a programme drafter and spokesman already experienced in argument and counter-argument. His first publications pointing the way for the future appeared in the mid-nineties in Brussels; from 1896 on his name was indissolubly linked with the concept 'l'Art Nouveau' (from an exhibition with this title at the gallery of S. Bing in Paris). On a trip to Germany in the winter of 1900/1 he proclaimed in *Kunstgewerblichen Laienpredigten* (Lay Sermons on Applied Art) his functional aesthetic, the aesthetic of 'pure form'. The publication of these lectures (Leipzig 1902) preceded the 'programme'.

To recognize the meaning, the form, the purpose of all the things of the material modern world with the same truth as the Greeks, among many others, recognized the meaning, form, and purpose of the column. It is not easy nowadays to find the exact meaning and the exact form for the simplest things.

It will take us a long time to recognize the exact form of a table, a chair, a house.

Religious, arbitrary, sentimental flights of fancy are parasitic plants.

As soon as the work of cleansing and sweeping out has been finished, as soon as the true form of things comes to light again, then strive with all the patience, all the spirit and the logic of the Greeks for the perfection of this form.

It seems to me that artistic sensibility is just as highly developed among ourselves as among the Greeks; what is less highly developed and weaker among ourselves, however, is the sense of perfection.

Under what social regime shall we enjoy the serenely transfigured calm that we need for work and for serious endeavour?
Answer:
Are we to expect from a *social* programme what can only spring *from our own most inward selves*?

Think rationally, cultivate artistic sensibility! Each one of us today can do this for himself; if only a large number of people do this a new social atmosphere will be brought about.

1906 Hans Poelzig:
Fermentation in architecture

During the period of his activity, Hans Poelzig (b.1869 in Berlin, d.1936 in Berlin) was link-man between the romantic-idealistic and radical-objective tendencies in the new architecture. We know his reflective, but at the same time incorruptible and exacting, judgment from his famous speech to the Bund Deutscher Architekten (Association of German Architects) on 4 June 1931. We also find it twenty-five years earlier in an essay on *Die Dritte Deutsche Kunstgewerbe-Ausstellung* (The Third German Exhibition of Applied Art, Dresden 1906). Poelzig, then head of the Academy of Arts in Breslau, makes it plain that there is more than just one step from applied art to architecture.

Essentially, the buildings at the Dresden Exhibition of Applied Art of 1906 mirror the process of fermentation which our architecture is today passing through, whose end cannot yet be foreseen and whose products are as yet scarcely to be recognized.

The main tasks of modern architecture do not lie in the ecclesiastical sphere, nor do monumental constructions of a secular character exercise a decisive influence. Life in the modern era is dominated by economic questions; thus the participation of the people and of artists in architectural problems of this kind – from the private dwelling to town planning – is constantly growing.

This is the starting point for most of the movements towards formalistic constructions, in so far as we can speak of a movement at a time marked by the multiplicity of vacillating trends – trends which for nearly a hundred years have been changing in quick succession the fundamental principles upon which they were based.

Attempts, mostly based on the art of Schinkel, to transpose elements of the Greek language of forms onto our buildings, were followed by an unselective use of forms taken from the most varied styles of the past – from Gothic via the Renaissance in both its Italian and its German manifestation to Baroque and Empire – generally with no regard for the inner spirit of the forms, with no regard for the material from which these forms originally sprang.

And isolated attempts by outstanding teachers of architecture in South and North Germany to attain by detailed study a knowledge of the artistic language of the ancients and its true meaning were soon crossed with energetic attempts to invent a new world language of architecture, whose rules and roots would not parallel or resemble any of the styles of the past.

And once again there is beginning a shamefaced revival of foreign words from architectural idioms belonging to many stylistic epochs, even primitive ones, and these foreign words are frequently grafted onto stems of fundamentally different character.

In almost all the subdivisions of art that serve decoration, with its simpler basic requirements, *the modern age has attained a genuine style of its own* and has splendid achievements to show. After initial vacillation there was a wholesome return – influenced by a study of the art of early times and especially of that of an Asian people – to techniques adapted to the material in question and an artistic elaboration of the motif based on a detailed study of nature.

Above all, wallpapers, textiles, glass windows, surface decoration, and minor arts of all kinds at the German Exhibition of Applied Art show this clearly enough, and architecture too demonstrates the decorative skill of its creators. But both the successful and the unsuccessful solutions clearly reveal that a true architecture is not to be achieved with the armoury of decoration, *that the problems of modern architecture cannot be mastered by purely external means.*

Flight from everything historical can no more bring salvation than a purely decorative return to forms from the past.

The principle of interpreting things in purely surface terms has for several decades led to shapes in various materials being reproduced according to a play of lines forced into a particular system – with no regard for scale. Apart from the great curtailment of inventiveness, this schematism may be harmless for small-scale works, but when applied to large-scale, tectonic projects it leads to monstrosities. It is partly as a result of recognizing this fact that we see so many instances of renunciation of any tectonic solution at all: supports remain shapeless and receive merely surface decoration, dividing cornices are omitted altogether.

This produces a tranquillity in the appearance of buildings that was often missing in the past, but it is a tranquillity applied by force, not the outcome of a real balance of energies accompanying full emphasis of the tectonic transitions. It is a frequent error of periods of fermentation to impose suddenly and forcibly developments that normally take several epochs to evolve, and to attempt to give a work an exceptional quality by applying external peculiarities that have not come into being organically and spontaneously. The artist's attention is distracted from what must be his main task: an unfailing mastery of his motif directly corresponding to his temperament and ability.

We also forget that the utilization of structures from earlier times for a building designed to meet the demands of modern life must be accompanied by an unmistakably modern adaptation of these structures, and that the correct use of materials and construction consciously adapted to purpose produce inner advantages that cannot be replaced by decorative embellishments, however skilfully applied.

We cannot do without the past in solving the architectural problems of our own day. We may dispense with the externals, but not with the work done in the past on the mastery of tectonic problems.

In spite of all the constructional achievements and changes, most of the best building materials are still the same and many of the constructions of the past remain unsurpassed. We are absolutely compelled to stay firmly planted on the shoulders of our forefathers and we deprive ourselves of a solid foothold if we begin *needlessly* to experiment afresh on our own account.

A sure eye and the right freedom in performing the tasks presented by the use of new building materials are to be acquired from a close study of what is possible and good for other materials and motifs. *This freedom has to be gained by an intellectual analysis and mastery of tradition and has nothing to do with that lack of restraint which inevitably leads to helpless confusion.*

The sad role frequently given to iron – that mighty aid to light structures and great spans – is that of a coupling which, because of its malleability and its ability to operate in concealment, is compelled to link together two elements in a building that are inorganically juxtaposed.

Every architectural work first has to tally with the work done by the engineer – and the modern architect more than any has no right to think illogically. But most of us are and remain sentimentalists and behave just as romantically as those who revived the formal elements of Gothic – not its tectonic core – around the middle of the nineteenth century. We all too frequently seek to save the emotional content of past epochs, without first thinking what use it is to us.

The past has bequeathed to us a deep understanding of materials and their characteristics, the evolution of science has afforded us a much more precise knowledge of the laws of statics, and yet for the most part we are more restricted and illogical in our thinking than was ever the case in an age that confronted architectonic problems armed only with sound common sense.

It is left to the engineer to calculate and design a unity between load and support, the right measurements for the parts of the structure consisting of various materials. The architect all too often seeks his salvation in purely decorative constructions that have to be imposed on the fabric of the building and spoil its organic clarity.

Every real tectonic constructional form has an absolute nucleus, to which the decorative embellishment, which within certain limits is changeable, lends a varying charm. First, however, the absolute element has to be found, even if as yet in an imperfect, rough form.

And the artist who approaches the design of structural elements solely from the viewpoint of external, decorative considerations distracts attention from the discovery of the pure nuclear form.

Domestic architecture is the first to begin freeing itself from an exterior conception, to make demands that operate from the inside outward, that help this architecture to achieve authenticity and have to be taken into account.

And yet here too the striving to say more than necessary often robs the building of that calm and naturalness which can be achieved by simplifying the overall design. Even here we are too much bogged down in an exterior, painterly conception and pay too little attention to the reconciliation between initially contradictory architectural demands (unity of material and form, limitation in the choice of materials) which creates tranquillity. Only when this overall tranquillity has been achieved does it become possible to apply decorative richness without overburdening the structure.

Instead, we often damage buildings of smaller dimension by attempting to increase their importance by stressing individual elements in a manner contrary to the organic harmony of the whole; we cannot go far enough in utilizing the most varied building materials in a single structure. And painterly play with emblems and applied decoration of all kinds, in so far as they serve no structural purpose, is merely confusing and easily leads to a mantle of sentimentality being thrown round a perfectly good basic structure, charming the undiscerning imitator and distracting his attention from the true core of the whole building.

The new movement carries the banner of objectivity against traditional structures that have become empty of content and petrified into a scheme. Objectivity is possible in architecture only on the basis of sound construction and a formal idiom evolved out of it.

Creative buildings of a new kind can come into being only in this way.

The fabric of our architectural idiom is still confused and we lack a knowledge of what is essential. We are still chasing after fashionable manners that after a short time, having been vulgarized by a series of imitators, become the object of contempt, whereas real architecture as the product of intense thought governed by artistic considerations offers little opportunity for unjustified robbery by imitators.

The right kind of architecture is already beginning to appear, especially in the case of buildings presenting few complications; here the path of unaffected artistic expression is already being trod. It is time to stop trying to make a style of this, to stop burdening the artist with the demand to evolve an intrusive personal note, which drives him to superficialities. For the time being we must demand only *unrelenting objectivity and a solution, in keeping with good taste, of a clearly thought out problem.*

1907 Henry van de Velde: Credo

In his book *Vom Neuen Stil* (On the New Style) Henry van de Velde continues the explanation of the principles set forth in his *Laienpredigten* (Lay Sermons). The three sections called by him *Credo* are to be found in the chapter entitled 'The Striving for a Style Based on a Rational, Logical Conception'. These principles, says Henry van de Velde, need only to be enunciated to be accepted as valid. Their fruitfulness has already been proved. In fact there arise from them the two basic demands not merely of the theory and critique of the new architecture, but also of its practice: honesty of materials, honesty of construction. Both have been till now uncontested.

Thou shalt comprehend the form and construction of all objects only in the sense of their strictest, elementary logic and justification for their existence.

Thou shalt adapt and subordinate these forms and constructions to the essential use of the material which thou employest.

And if thou art animated by the wish to beautify these forms and constructions, give thyself to the longing for refinement to which thy aesthetic sensibility or taste for ornament – of whatever kind it is –

shall inspire thee, only so far as thou canst respect and retain the rights and the essential appearance of these forms and constructions!

1908 Adolf Loos:
Ornament and crime

Adolf Loos (b.1870 in Brno, d.1933 in Vienna) brought back with him to Vienna
from his three-year stay in the United States (1893–6) a remark of Louis
Sullivan's: 'It could only benefit us if for a time we were to abandon ornament
and concentrate entirely on the erection of buildings that were finely shaped
and charming in their sobriety'.
From this Loos developed his radical aesthetic purism, which made him a
zealous foe of Art Nouveau and the German Werkbund: 'The German
Werkbund has set out to discover the style of our age. This is unnecessary
labour. We already have the style of our age.'

The human embryo in the womb passes through all the evolutionary stages
of the animal kingdom. When man is born, his sensory impressions are
like those of a newborn puppy. His childhood takes him through all the
metamorphoses of human history. At 2 he sees with the eyes of a Papuan, at 4
with those of an ancient Teuton, at 6 with those of Socrates, at 8 with those
of Voltaire. When he is 8 he becomes aware of violet, the colour discovered
by the eighteenth century, because before that the violet was blue and the
purple-snail red. The physicist points today to colours in the solar spectrum
which already have a name but the knowledge of which is reserved for the
men of the future.

The child is amoral. To our eyes, the Papuan is too. The Papuan kills his
enemies and eats them. He is not a criminal. But when modern man kills
someone and eats him he is either a criminal or a degenerate. The Papuan
tattoos his skin, his boat, his paddles, in short everything he can lay hands on.
He is not a criminal. The modern man who tattoos himself is either a criminal
or a degenerate. There are prisons in which eighty per cent of the inmates
show tattoos. The tattooed who are not in prison are latent criminals or
degenerate aristocrats. If someone who is tattooed dies at liberty, it means he
has died a few years before committing a murder.

The urge to ornament one's face and everything within reach is the start of
plastic art. It is the baby talk of painting. All art is erotic.

The first ornament that was born, the cross, was erotic in origin. The first
work of art, the first artistic act which the first artist, in order to rid himself of
his surplus energy, smeared on the wall. A horizontal dash: the prone woman.
A vertical dash: the man penetrating her. The man who created it felt the
same urge as Beethoven, he was in the same heaven in which Beethoven
created the *Ninth Symphony*.

But the man of our day who, in response to an inner urge, smears the walls
with erotic symbols is a criminal or a degenerate. It goes without saying that
this impulse most frequently assails people with such symptoms of degeneracy
in the lavatory. A country's culture can be assessed by the extent to which its
lavatory walls are smeared. In the child this is a natural phenomenon: his

first artistic expression is to scribble erotic symbols on the walls. But what is natural to the Papuan and the child is a symptom of degeneracy in the modern adult. I have made the following discovery and I pass it on to the world: *The evolution of culture is synonymous with the removal of ornament from utilitarian objects.* I believed that with this discovery I was bringing joy to the world; it has not thanked me. People were sad and hung their heads. What depressed them was the realization that they could produce no new ornaments. Are we alone, the people of the nineteenth century, supposed to be unable to do what any Negro, all the races and periods before us have been able to do? What mankind created without ornament in earlier millenia was thrown away without a thought and abandoned to destruction. We possess no joiner's benches from the Carolingian era, but every trifle that displays the least ornament has been collected and cleaned and palatial buildings have been erected to house it. Then people walked sadly about between the glass cases and felt ashamed of their impotence. Every age had its style, is our age alone to be refused a style? By style, people meant ornament. Then I said: Weep not! See, therein lies the greatness of our age, that it is incapable of producing a new ornament. We have outgrown ornament; we have fought our way through to freedom from ornament. See, the time is nigh, fulfilment awaits us. Soon the streets of the city will glisten like white walls. Like Zion, the holy city, the capital of heaven. Then fulfilment will be come.

There were black albs, clerical gentlemen, who wouldn't put up with that. Mankind was to go on panting in slavery to ornament. Men had gone far enough for ornament no longer to arouse feelings of pleasure in them, far enough for a tattooed face not to heighten the aesthetic effect, as among the Papuans, but to reduce it. Far enough to take pleasure in a plain cigarette case, whereas an ornamented one, even at the same price, was not bought. They were happy in their clothes and glad they didn't have to go around in red velvet hose with gold braid like fairground monkeys. And I said: See, Goethe's death-chamber is finer than all Renaissance splendour and a plain piece of furniture more beautiful than any inlaid and carved museum pieces. Goethe's language is finer than all the ornaments of Pegnitz's shepherds.

The black albs heard this with displeasure, and the state, whose task it is to halt the cultural development of the peoples, made the question of the development and revival of ornament its own. Woe to the state whose revolutions are in the care of the *Hofrats*! Very soon we saw in the Wiener Kunstgewerbemuseum [Vienna Museum of Applied Art] a sideboard known as 'the rich haul of fish', soon there were cupboards bearing the name 'the enchanted princess' or something similar referring to the ornament with which this unfortunate piece of furniture was covered. The Austrian state took its task so seriously that it is making sure the foot-rags used on the frontiers of the Austro-Hungarian monarchy do not disappear. It is forcing every cultivated man of 20 for three years to wear foot-rags instead of manufactured footwear. After all, every state starts from the premise that a people on a lower footing is easier to rule.

Very well, the ornament disease is recognized by the state and subsidized with state funds. But I see in this a retrograde step. I don't accept the objection that ornament heightens a cultivated person's joy in life, don't accept the objection contained in the words: 'But if the ornament is beautiful!' Ornament does not heighten my joy in life or the joy in life of any cultivated person. If I want to eat a piece of gingerbread I choose one that is quite smooth and not a piece representing a heart or a baby or a rider, which is covered all over with ornaments. The man of the fifteenth century won't understand me. But all modern people will. The advocate of ornament believes that my urge for simplicity is in the nature of a mortification. No, respected professor at the school of applied art, I am not mortifying myself! The show dishes of past centuries, which display all kinds of ornaments to make the peacocks, pheasants and lobsters look more tasty, have exactly the opposite effect on me. I am horrified when I go through a cookery exhibition and think that I am meant to eat these stuffed carcasses. I eat roast beef.

The enormous damage and devastation caused in aesthetic development by the revival of ornament would be easily made light of, for no one, not even the power of the state, can halt mankind's evolution. It can only be delayed. We can wait. But it is a crime against the national economy that it should result in a waste of human labour, money, and material. Time cannot make good this damage.

The speed of cultural evolution is reduced by the stragglers. I perhaps am living in 1908, but my neighbour is living in 1900 and the man across the way in 1880. It is unfortunate for a state when the culture of its inhabitants is spread over such a great period of time. The peasants of Kals are living in the twelfth century. And there were peoples taking part in the Jubilee parade [of the Emperor Franz Joseph] who would have been considered backward even during the migration of the nations. Happy the land that has no such stragglers and marauders. Happy America!

Among ourselves there are unmodern people even in the cities, stragglers from the eighteenth century, who are horrified by a picture with purple shadows because they cannot yet see purple. The pheasant on which the chef has been working all day long tastes better to them and they prefer the cigarette case with Renaissance ornaments to the smooth one. And what is it like in the country? Clothes and household furniture all belong to past centuries. The peasant isn't a Christian, he is still a pagan.

The stragglers slow down the cultural evolution of the nations and of mankind; not only is ornament produced by criminals but also a crime is committed through the fact that ornament inflicts serious injury on people's health, on the national budget and hence on cultural evolution. If two people live side by side with the same needs, the same demands on life and the same income but belonging to different cultures, economically speaking the following process can be observed: the twentieth-century man will get richer and richer, the eighteenth-century man poorer and poorer. I am assuming that both live according to their inclinations. The twentieth-century man can satisfy his needs with a far lower capital outlay and hence can save money. The vegetable he enjoys is simply boiled in water and has a little butter put on it. The other man likes it equally well only when honey and nuts have been added to it and someone has spent hours cooking it. Ornamented plates are very expensive, whereas the white crockery from which the modern man likes to eat is cheap. The one accumulates savings, the other debts. It is the same with whole nations. Woe when a people remains behind in cultural evolution! The British are growing wealthier and we poorer . . .

Even greater is the damage done by ornament to the nation that produces it. Since ornament is no longer a natural product of our culture, so that it is a phenomenon either of backwardness or degeneration, the work of the ornamentor is no longer adequately remunerated.

The relationship between the earnings of a woodcarver and a turner, the criminally low wages paid to the embroideress and the lacemaker are well known. The ornamentor has to work twenty hours to achieve the income earned by a modern worker in eight. Ornament generally increases the cost of an article; nevertheless it happens that an ornamented object whose raw material cost the same and which demonstrably took three times as long to make is offered at half the price of a smooth object. Omission of ornament results in a reduction in the manufacturing time and an increase in wages. The Chinese carver works for sixteen hours, the American worker for eight. If I pay as much for a smooth cigarette case as for an ornamented one, the difference in the working time belongs to the worker. And if there were no ornament at all – a situation that may perhaps come about in some thousands of years – man would only have to work four hours instead of eight, because half of the work done today is devoted to ornament. Ornament is wasted labour power and hence wasted health. It has always been so.

Since ornament is no longer organically linked with our culture, it is also no longer the expression of our culture. The ornament that is manufactured today has no connexion with us, has absolutely no human connexions, no connexion with the world order. It is not capable of developing. What happened to Otto Eckmann's ornament, or van de Velde's? The artist has always stood at the forefront of mankind full of vigour and health. But the modern ornamentalist is a straggler or a pathological phenomenon. He himself will repudiate his own products three years later. To cultivated people they are immediately intolerable; others become aware of their intolerable character only years later. Where are Otto Eckmann's works today? Modern ornament has no parents and no progeny, no past and no future. By uncultivated people, to whom the grandeur of our age is a book with seven seals, it is greeted joyfully and shortly afterwards repudiated.

Mankind is healthier than ever; only a few people are sick. But these few tyrannize over the worker who is so healthy that he cannot invent ornament. They force him to execute in the most varied materials the ornaments which they have invented.

Changes of ornament lead to a premature devaluation of the labour product. The worker's time and the material employed are capital goods that are wasted. I have stated the proposition: the form of an object lasts, that is to say remains tolerable, as long as the object lasts physically. I will try to explain this. A suit will change its form more often than a valuable fur. A lady's ball gown, intended for only one night, will change its form more quickly than a desk. But woe if a desk has to be changed as quickly as a ball gown because the old form has become intolerable; in that case the money spent on the desk will have been lost.

This is well known to the ornamentalist, and Austrian ornamentalists are trying to make the best of this shortcoming. They say: 'We prefer a consumer who has a set of furniture that becomes intolerable to him after ten years, and who is consequently forced to refurnish every ten years, to one who only buys an object when the old one is worn out. Industry demands this. Millions are employed as a result of the quick change.'

This seems to be the secret of the Austrian national economy. How often do we hear someone say when there is a fire: 'Thank God, now there will be work for people to do again.' In that case I know a splendid solution. Set fire to a town, set fire to the empire, and everyone will be swimming in money and prosperity. Manufacture furniture which after three years can be used for firewood, metal fittings that have to be melted down after four years because even at an auction sale it is impossible to get a tenth of the original value of the material and labour, and we shall grow wealthier and wealthier.

The loss does not hit only the consumer; above all it hits the producer. Today ornament on things that have evolved away from the need to be ornamented represents wasted labour and ruined material. If all objects would last aesthetically as long as they do physically, the consumer could pay a price for them that would enable the worker to earn more money and work shorter hours. For an object I am sure I can use to its full extent I willingly pay four times as much as for one that is inferior in form or material. I happily pay forty kronen for my boots, although in a different shop I could get boots for ten kronen. But in those trades that groan under the tyranny of the ornamentalist no distinction is made between good and bad workmanship. The work suffers because no one is willing to pay its true value.

And this is a good thing, because these ornamented objects are tolerable only when they are of the most miserable quality. I get over a fire much more easily when I hear that only worthless trash has been burned. I can be pleased about the trash in the Künstlerhaus because I know that it will be manufactured in a few days and taken to pieces in one. But throwing gold coins instead of stones, lighting a cigarette with a banknote, pulverizing and drinking a pearl create an unaesthetic effect.

Ornamented things first create a truly unaesthetic effect when they have been executed in the best material and with the greatest care and have taken long hours of labour. I cannot exonerate myself from having initially demanded quality work, but naturally not for that kind of thing.

The modern man who holds ornament sacred as a sign of the artistic superabundance of past ages will immediately recognize the tortured, strained, and morbid quality of modern ornaments. No ornament can any longer be made today by anyone who lives on our cultural level.

It is different with the individuals and peoples who have not yet reached this level.

I am preaching to the aristocrat, I mean the person who stands at the pinnacle of mankind and yet has the deepest understanding for the distress and want of those below. He well understands the Kaffir who weaves ornaments into his fabric according to a particular rhythm that only comes into view when it is unravelled, the Persian who weaves his carpet, the Slovak peasant woman who embroiders her lace, the old lady who crochets wonderful things with glass beads and silk. The aristocrat lets them be; he knows that the hours in which they work are their holy hours. The revolutionary would go to them and say: 'It's all nonsense.' Just as he would pull down the little old woman from the wayside crucifix and tell her: 'There is no God.' The atheist among the aristocrats, on the other hand, raises his hat when he passes a church.

My shoes are covered all over with ornaments consisting of scallops and holes. Work done by the shoemaker for which he was never paid. I go to the shoemaker and say: 'You ask thirty kronen for a pair of shoes. I will pay you forty kronen.' I have thereby raised this man to heights of bliss for which he will thank me by work and material infinitely better than would be called for by the additional price. He is happy. Happiness rarely enters his house. Here is a man who understands him, who values his work and does not doubt his honesty. He already sees the finished shoes in his mind's eye. He knows where the best leather is to be found at the present time; he knows which craftsman he will entrust the shoes to; and the shoes will be so covered in scallops and holes as only an elegant shoe can be. And then I say to him: 'But there's one condition. The shoes must be completely smooth.' With this I have cast him down from the heights of bliss to the pit of despondency. He has less work, but I have taken away all his joy.

I am preaching to the aristocrat. I tolerate ornaments on my own body, when they constitute the joy of my fellow men. Then they are my joy too. I can tolerate the ornaments of the Kaffir, the Persian, the Slovak peasant woman, my shoemaker's ornaments, for they all have no other way of attaining the high points of their existence. We have art, which has taken the place of ornament. After the toils and troubles of the day we go to Beethoven or to Tristan. This my shoemaker cannot do. I mustn't deprive him of his joy, since I have nothing else to put in its place. But anyone who goes to the *Ninth Symphony* and then sits down and designs a wallpaper pattern is either a confidence trickster or a degenerate. Absence of ornament has brought the other arts to unsuspected heights. Beethoven's symphonies would never have been written by a man who had to walk about in silk, satin, and lace. Anyone who goes around in a velvet coat today is not an artist but a buffoon or a house painter. We have grown finer, more subtle. The nomadic herdsmen had to distinguish themselves by various colours; modern man uses his clothes as a mask. So immensely strong is his individuality that it can no longer be expressed in articles of clothing. Freedom from ornament is a sign of spiritual strength. Modern man uses the ornaments of earlier or alien cultures as he sees fit. He concentrates his own inventiveness on other things.

1910   Frank Lloyd Wright:
Organic architecture (excerpt)

In 1910 Frank Lloyd Wright (b.1867 or 1869 in Richland Center, Wisconsin, d.1959 in Taliesin West, Arizona) came to Germany at the invitation of the publisher Ernst Wasmuth in order to supervise the first publication of his *Collected Works* (1893–1910). Kuno Franck, for some time an exchange professor at Harvard, had drawn attention to Wright in Berlin. With this publication, for which Wright himself wrote an introduction, the architectural idea of a free spatial flow between the various dwelling-areas, and the organic development of a building on an L-, X-, or T-shaped ground plan gained a firm foothold in Europe.

In Organic Architecture then, it is quite impossible to consider the building as one thing, its furnishings another and its setting and environment still another. The Spirit in which these buildings are conceived sees all these together at work as one thing. All are to be studiously foreseen and provided for in the nature of the structure. All these should become mere details of the character and completeness of the structure. Incorporated (or excluded) are lighting, heating and ventilation. The very chairs and tables, cabinets and even musical instruments, where practicable, are of the building itself, never fixtures upon it . . .

To thus make of a human dwelling-place a complete work of art, in itself expressive and beautiful, intimately related to modern life and fit to live in, lending itself more freely and suitably to the individual needs of the dwellers as itself an harmonious entity, fitting in colour, pattern and nature the utilities and be really an expression of them in character, – this is the tall modern American opportunity in Architecture. True basis of a true Culture. An exalted view to take of the 'property instinct' of our times? But once founded and on view I believe this Ideal will become a new Tradition: a vast step in advance of the prescribed fashion in a day when a dwelling was a composite of cells arranged as separate rooms: chambers to contain however good aggregations of furniture, utility comforts not present: a property interest chiefly. An organic-entity, this modern building as contrasted with that former insensate aggregation of parts. Surely we have here the higher ideal of unity as a more intimate working out of the expression of one's life in one's environment. One great thing instead of a quarrelling collection of so many little things.

1911   Hermann Muthesius:
Aims of the Werkbund (excerpt)

The true occasion of the birth of the Deutscher Werkbund (German Arts and Crafts Society) was the Third German Exhibition of Applied Art in Dresden in 1906. The proposal of certain friends who shared the same outlook that 'the exhibition should end in the founding of a society of artists and highly qualified representatives of trade and industry' was put into practice on 6 October 1907. Although one of the movers of this proposal, Hermann Muthesius (b.1861 in Gross-Neuhausen, d.1927 in Berlin) was not among the founder members. Nevertheless Muthesius was the first to formulate the society's programme. As a result of his reports on British domestic architecture (1904–7), however, he was already known to the German arts and crafts movement and building industry as 'The Muthesius Case'.

To help form to recover its rights must be the fundamental task of our era; in particular it must be the content of any work of artistic reform embarked upon today. The fortunate progress of the arts and crafts movement, which has given new shape to the interior decoration of our rooms, breathed fresh life into handicrafts and imparted fruitful inspiration to architecture, may be regarded as only a minor prelude to what must come. For in spite of all we have achieved we are still wading up to our knees in the brutalization of forms. If proof is needed, we have only to observe the fact that our country is being covered daily and hourly with buildings of the most inferior character, unworthy of our age and calculated to speak to posterity all too eloquently of our epoch's lack of culture. What sense is there in speaking of success so long as this is still the case? Is there a more accurate testimony to a nation's taste than the buildings with which it fills its streets and populated areas? What would it mean, compared with this, if we could prove that today the energies required for decent architectural constructions are available and that these energies have simply not been able to get to grips with the tasks? Precisely the fact that they have not got to grips with the tasks characterizes the cultural situation of our day. The very fact that thousands and thousands of our people not merely pass by this crime against form unperturbed, but as the employers of architects contribute to its multiplication by choosing unsuitable advisers, is unmistakable proof of the abysmal condition of our sense of form and hence of our artistic culture in general.

The Deutscher Werkbund was founded in years when a closing of the ranks of all those struggling for better things was made necessary by the violent assaults of their opponents. Its years of struggle for its principles are now over. The ideas it existed to propagate are no longer contradicted by anyone; they enjoy universal acceptance. Does this mean that its existence is now superfluous? One might think so if one were to consider only the narrower field of applied art. But we cannot rest content with having put cushions and chairs in order; we must think further. In truth the Deutscher Werkbund's real work is only now beginning, with the dawning of the era of peace. And if up to now the idea of quality has held first place in the Werkbund's work we can already observe today that, as far as technique and material are concerned, the sense of quality in Germany is in the process of rapidly improving. Yet even this success is far from completing the Werkbund's task. Far more important than the material aspect is the spiritual; higher than purpose, material, and technique stands form. Purpose, material, and technique might be beyond criticism, yet without form we should still be living in a crude and brutal world. Thus we are ever more clearly confronted by the far greater, far more important task of reviving intellectual understanding and reanimating the architectonic sense. For its architectonic culture is and remains the true index of a nation's culture as a whole. If a nation produces good furniture and good light fittings, but daily erects the worst possible buildings, this can only be a sign of heterogeneous, unclarified conditions, conditions whose very inconsistency is proof of the lack of discipline and organization. Without a total respect for form, culture is unthinkable, and formlessness is synonymous with lack of culture. Form is a higher spiritual need to the same degree that cleanliness is a higher bodily need. Crudities of form cause the really cultivated man an almost physical pain; in their presence he has the same feeling of discomfort produced by dirt and a bad smell. But as long as a sense of form has not been developed in the cultured members of our nation to the same level of intensity as their need for clean linen, we are still far removed from conditions which could in any way be compared with epochs of high cultural achievement.

1914   Muthesius/Van de Velde:
Werkbund theses and antitheses

In June 1914 the first great exhibition of the Deutscher Werkbund was opened
in Cologne. It was intended to provide a conspectus of the Werkbund's work in
the seven years since its foundation. The very heterogeneity of the buildings in
the exhibition – ranging from the Neo-Classicism of a Behrens to the gaily
austere objectivity of Gropius and Meyer's office building and factory – gives a
hint of the opposing forces within the Werkbund. They clashed with full vigour
at the Werkbund conference in Cologne at the beginning of July, when
Muthesius proclaimed concentration and standardization as the aims of
Werkbund design, while van de Velde advanced the contrary thesis of the
artist as a creative individualist.

1. Architecture, and with it the whole area of the Werkbund's activities, is
pressing towards standardization, and only through standardization can it
recover that universal significance which was characteristic of it in times of
harmonious culture.

2. Standardization, to be understood as the result of a beneficial concentration, will alone make possible the development of a universally valid, unfailing good taste.

3. As long as a universal high level of taste has not been achieved, we cannot
count on German arts and crafts making their influence effectively felt abroad.

4. The world will demand our products only when they are the vehicles of a
convincing stylistic expression. The foundations for this have now been laid
by the German movement.

5. The creative development of what has already been achieved is the most
urgent task of the age. Upon it the movement's ultimate success will depend.
Any relapse and deterioration into imitation would today mean the squander-
ing of a valuable possession.

6. Starting from the conviction that it is a matter of life and death for Germany constantly to ennoble its production, the Deutscher Werkbund, as an
association of artists, industrialists, and merchants, must concentrate its
attention upon creating the preconditions for the export of its industrial arts.

7. Germany's advances in applied art and architecture must be brought to the
attention of foreign countries by effective publicity. Next to exhibitions the
most obvious means of doing this is by periodical illustrated publications.

8. Exhibitions by the Deutscher Werkbund are only meaningful when they

are restricted radically to the best and most exemplary. Exhibitions of arts and crafts abroad must be looked upon as a national matter and hence require public subsidy.

9. The existence of efficient large-scale business concerns with reliable good taste is a prerequisite of any export. It would be impossible to meet even internal demands with an object designed by the artist for individual requirements.

10. For national reasons large distributive and transport undertakings whose activities are directed abroad ought to link up with the new movement, now that it has shown what it can do, and consciously represent German art in the world.

Hermann Muthesius

1. So long as there are still artists in the Werkbund and so long as they exercise some influence on its destiny, they will protest against every suggestion for the establishment of a canon and for standardization. By his innermost essence the artist is a burning idealist, a free spontaneous creator. Of his own free will he will never subordinate himself to a discipline that imposes upon him a type, a canon. Instinctively he distrusts everything that might sterilize his actions, and everyone who preaches a rule that might prevent him from thinking his thoughts through to their own free end, or that attempts to drive him into a universally valid form, in which he sees only a mask that seeks to make a virtue out of incapacity.

2. Certainly, the artist who practises a 'beneficial concentration' has always recognized that currents which are stronger than his own will and thought demand of him that he should acknowledge what is in essential correspondence to the spirit of his age. These currents may be very manifold; he absorbs them unconsciously and consciously as general influences; there is something materially and morally compelling about them for him. He willingly subordinates himself to them and is full of enthusiasm for the idea of a new style *per se*. And for twenty years many of us have been seeking forms and decorations entirely in keeping with our epoch.

3. Nevertheless it has not occurred to any of us that henceforth we ought to try to impose these forms and decorations, which we have sought or found, upon others as standards. We know that several generations will have to work upon what we have started before the physiognomy of the new style is established, and that we can talk of standards and standardization only after the passage of a whole period of endeavours.

4. But we also know that as long as this goal has not been reached our

endeavours will still have the charm of creative impetus. Gradually the energies, the gifts of all, begin to combine together, antitheses become neutralized, and at precisely that moment when individual strivings begin to slacken, the physiognomy will be established. The era of imitation will begin and forms and decorations will be used, the production of which no longer calls for any creative impulse: the age of infertility will then have commenced.

5. The desire to see a standard type come into being before the establishment of a style is exactly like wanting to see the effect before the cause. It would be to destroy the embryo in the egg. Is anyone really going to let themselves be dazzled by the apparent possibility of thereby achieving quick results? These premature effects have all the less prospect of enabling German arts and crafts to exercise an effective influence abroad, because foreign countries are a jump ahead of us in the old tradition and the old culture of good taste.

6. Germany, on the other hand, has the great advantage of still possessing gifts which other, older, wearier peoples are losing: the gifts of invention, of brilliant personal brainwaves. And it would be nothing short of castration to tie down this rich, many-sided, creative élan so soon.

7. The efforts of the Werkbund should be directed toward cultivating precisely these gifts, as well as the gifts of individual manual skill, joy, and belief in the beauty of highly differentiated execution, not toward inhibiting them by standardization at the very moment when foreign countries are beginning to take an interest in German work. As far as fostering these gifts is concerned, almost everything still remains to be done.

8. We do not deny anyone's good will and we are very well aware of the difficulties that have to be overcome in carrying this out. We know that the workers' organization has done a very great deal for the workers' material welfare, but it can hardly find an excuse for having done so little towards arousing enthusiasm for consummately fine workmanship in those who ought to be our most joyful collaborators. On the other hand, we are well aware of the need to export that lies like a curse upon our industry.

9. And yet nothing, nothing good and splendid, was ever created out of mere consideration for exports. Quality will not be created out of the spirit of export. Quality is always first created exclusively for a quite limited circle of connoisseurs and those who commission the work. These gradually gain confidence in their artists; slowly there develops first a narrower, then a national clientele, and only then do foreign countries, does the world slowly take notice of this quality. It is a complete misunderstanding of the situation to make the industrialists believe that they would increase their chances in the world market if they produced *a priori* standardized types for this world market before these types had become well tried common property at home. The wonderful works being exported to us now were none of them originally

created for export: think of Tiffany glasses, Copenhagen porcelain, jewellery by Jensen, the books of Cobden-Sanderson, and so on.

10. Every exhibition must have as its purpose to show the world this native quality, and it is quite true that the Werkbund's exhibitions will have meaning only when, as Herr Muthesius so rightly says, they restrict themselves radically to the best and most exemplary.

Henry van de Velde

1914 Paul Scheerbart:
Glass architecture (excerpt)

The architect Bruno Taut called Paul Scheerbart (b.1863 in Danzig, d.1915 in Berlin) the 'only poet in architecture'. Scheerbart's Utopian phantasmagoria, which he wrote in marvellous abundance from 1893 on, evokes more impressively each time the idea of a 'glass architecture', the architect's dream of light, crystal clear, colourful, mobile, floating and soaring constructions that will transform 'Old Europe's' habits of thought and feeling. In 1914, the same year in which Bruno Taut, inspired by Scheerbart, built his 'Glass House' at the Werkbund Exhibition in Cologne, Herwarth Walden printed Scheerbart's 111-chapter 'Glass Architecture' in *Sturm*.

I. The environment and its influence on the evolution of culture
We live for the most part within enclosed spaces. These form the environment from which our culture grows. Our culture is in a sense a product of our architecture. If we wish to raise our culture to a higher level, we are forced for better or for worse to transform our architecture. And this will be possible only if we remove the enclosed quality from the spaces within which we live. This can be done only through the introduction of glass architecture that lets the sunlight and the light of the moon and stars into our rooms not merely through a few windows, but simultaneously through the greatest possible number of walls that are made entirely of glass – coloured glass. The new environment that we shall thereby create must bring with it a new culture.

XVIII. The beauty of the Earth if glass architecture is everywhere
The surface of the Earth would change greatly if brick architecture were everywhere displaced by glass architecture.

It would be as though the Earth clad itself in jewellery of brilliants and enamel.

The splendour is absolutely unimaginable. And we should then have on the Earth more exquisite things than the gardens of the Arabian Nights.

Then we should have a paradise on Earth and would not need to gaze longingly at the paradise in the sky.

XLI. The possibilities which iron construction renders capable of development
Iron construction makes it possible to give walls any form that may be desired. Walls need no longer be vertical.

Hence the possibilities which iron construction enables to be developed are quite unlimited.

The dome effects up above can be displaced to the sides, so that when sitting at a table one need only look sideways and upwards in order to observe the dome effect.

But curved surfaces are also effective in the lower parts of the walls – this effect is particularly easy to achieve in smaller rooms.

Smaller rooms are totally and completely freed from the need for verticality.

The significance of the ground-plan in architecture is thereby greatly reduced; the design of the outline of the building acquires greater importance than hitherto.

LXII. The terraces
No doubt a terrace formation is necessary in taller glass buildings and with several storeys, since otherwise the glass surfaces could not reach the free light-conducting air, to which they aspire, since in darkness they can fulfil their purpose only at night – not during the day.

This terrace formation of the storeys will of course quickly replace the dreary frontal architecture of brick houses.

LXXI. Transportable buildings
Transportable glass buildings can also be manufactured. They are particularly well suited for exhibition purposes.

Such transportable buildings are not exactly easy to produce. But let it not be forgotten that when something new is involved it is very often precisely the most difficult problem that is tackled first.

CII. The transformation of the Earth's surface
Again and again something sounds to us like a fairy tale, when it is not really so fantastic or Utopian at all. Eighty years ago the steam railway came along and actually transformed the whole surface of the Earth, as no one will deny.

According to what has been said so far the surface of the Earth is to be transformed – and by glass architecture. If it comes, it will transform the Earth's surface. Naturally, a part will also be played by other factors outside the present discussion.

It was the steam railway that produced the brick metropolis culture of today from which we all suffer. Glass architecture will come only when the metropolis in our sense of the word has been done away with.

That it must be done away with is perfectly clear to all those who aim at the further evolution of our culture. This is no longer worth talking about.

We all know what colour means; it forms only a small part of the spectrum. But this we want to have. Infra-red and ultra-violet are not perceptible to our eyes – but no doubt ultra-violet is perceptible to the sense organs of ants.

Even if we cannot for the present assume that our sense organs will evolve further from today to tomorrow, we shall nevertheless be justified in supposing that to begin with we may attain that which is accessible to us – to wit, that part of the spectrum which we are able to perceive with our eyes, those miracles of colour which we are capable of taking in.

The only thing that can help us to do this is glass architecture, which must transform our whole life – the environment in which we live.

It is therefore to be hoped that glass architecture really will 'transform' the surface of our Earth.

1914 Antonio Sant'Elia/Filippo Tommaso Marinetti: Futurist architecture

In 1914 two young architects, Antonio Sant'Elia and Mario Chiattone, exhibited in Milan drawings and plans for a 'New City'. The radical ideas put forward by Antonio Sant'Elia (b.1888 in Como, killed 1916 at Monfalcone) in the foreword to the catalogue were immediately reinterpreted by Marinetti, the mouthpiece of Italian Futurism, into a 'Manifesto of Futurist Architecture', which appeared in July of the same year, four months after Marinetti's manifesto *The Splendour of Geometry and Mechanics and the Sensibility of Numbers*, and concluded the series of great Futurist proclamations.

The words and passages in italics were added to Sant'Elia's statement by Marinetti and Cinti.

Since the eighteenth century there has been no more architecture. What is called modern architecture is a stupid mixture of the most varied stylistic elements used to mask the modern skeleton. The new beauty of concrete and iron is profaned by the superimposition of carnival decorative incrustations justified neither by structural necessity nor by our taste, and having their origins in Egyptian, Indian or Byzantine antiquity or in that astounding outburst of idiocies and impotence known as 'neo-classicism'.

In Italy these products of architectural pandering are welcomed, and greedy incompetence from abroad is rated as brilliant inventiveness, as the very latest architecture. Young Italian architects (those who gain a reputation for originality through the clandestine machinations of art magazines) display their talents in the new quarters of our cities, where a joyful confusion of ogival columns, seventeenth-century foliage, Gothic arches, Egyptian pilasters, rococo volutes, fifteenth-century putti and bloated caryatids seriously claim to be regarded as style and arrogantly strive for monumentality. The kaleidoscopic appearance and disappearance of forms, the constantly growing number of machines, the daily increase of needs imposed by the speed of communications, by the agglomeration of people, by the demands of hygiene and a hundred other phenomena of modern life, cause no concern to these self-styled renewers of architecture. They stubbornly continue to apply the rules of Vitruvius, Vignola and Sansovino and with a few little German architectural publications in their hands try to re-impose age-old imbecilities upon our cities, which ought to be the direct and faithful projections of ourselves.

Thus this art of expression and synthesis has become in their hands an empty stylistic exercise, an endless repetition of formulas incompetently employed to disguise as a modern building the usual hackneyed conglomeration of bricks and stones. As though we – the accumulators and generators of movement, with our mechanical extensions, with the noise and speed of our life – could live in the same streets built for their own needs by the men of four, five, six centuries ago.

This is the supreme idiocy of the modern architecture that constantly repeats itself with the self-interested complicity of the academies, those prisons of the intelligence in which the young are forced onanistically to copy classical models, instead of opening up their minds to the search for limits and the solution of the new and imperious problem: 'the Futurist house and city'. The house and the city spiritually and materially ours, in which our turbulent existence can take place without appearing a grotesque anachronism.

The problem of *Futurist* architecture is not a problem of linear rearrangement. It is not a question of finding new profiles, new door and window frames, substitutes for columns, pilasters, consoles, caryatids, gargoyles. It is not a question of leaving the façade bare brick, painting it or facing it with stone; nor of establishing formal differences between new and old buildings. It is a question of creating the *Futurist* house according to a sound plan, of building it with the aid of every scientific and technical resource, of fulfilling to the limit every demand of our way of life and our spirit, of rejecting everything grotesque, cumbrous, and alien to us (tradition, style, aesthetic, proportion), establishing new forms, new lines, *a new harmony of profiles and volumes*, an architecture whose raison d'être lies solely in the special conditions of modern life, whose aesthetic values are in perfect harmony with our sensibility. This architecture cannot be subject to any law of historical continuity. It must be as new as our frame of mind is new.

The art of building has been able to evolve in time and to pass from one style to another while maintaining the general characteristics of architecture unaltered, because, while changes due to fashion and those resulting from successive religious movements and political regimes are frequent in history, factors that cause profound changes in environmental conditions, that overturn the old and create the new – such things as the discovery of natural laws, the perfecting of mechanical systems, the rational and scientific use of material – are very rare indeed. In modern times, the process of the consistent stylistic evolution of architecture has come to a stop. 'Architecture is breaking free from tradition. It must perforce begin again from the beginning.'

The calculation of the strength of materials, the use of reinforced concrete, rule out 'architecture' in the classical and traditional sense. Modern building materials and our scientific ideas absolutely do not lend themselves to the disciplines of historical styles and are the chief cause of the grotesque appearance of buildings à la mode, in which an attempt is made to force the splendidly light and slender supporting members and the apparent fragility of reinforced concrete to imitate the heavy curve of arches and the massive appearance of marble.

The tremendous antithesis between the modern and the ancient world is the outcome of all those things that exist now and did not exist then. Elements have entered into our life of whose very possibility the ancients did not even dream. Material possibilities and attitudes of mind have come into being that have had a thousand repercussions, first and foremost of which is the creation of a new ideal of beauty, still obscure and embryonic, but whose fascination is already being felt even by the masses. We have lost the sense of the monumental, of the heavy, of the static; we have enriched our sensibility by a 'taste for the light, the practical, *the ephemeral and the swift*'. We feel that we are no longer the men of the cathedrals, *the palaces,* the assembly halls; but of big hotels, railway stations, immense roads, colossal ports, covered markets, brilliantly lit galleries, freeways, demolition and rebuilding schemes.

We must invent and rebuild the *Futurist* city: it must be like an immense, tumultuous, lively, noble work site, dynamic in all its parts; and the *Futurist* house must be like an enormous machine. The lifts must not hide like lonely worms in the stair wells; the stairs, become useless, must be done away with and the lifts must climb like serpents of iron and glass up the housefronts. The house of concrete, glass, and iron, *without painting* and without sculpture, enriched solely by the innate beauty of its lines and projections, extremely 'ugly' in its mechanical simplicity, high and wide *as prescribed by local government regulations,* must rise on the edge of a tumultuous abyss: the street, which will no longer stretch like a foot-mat level with the porters' lodges, but will descend into the earth on several levels, will receive the metropolitan traffic and will be linked, for the necessary passage from one to the other, by metal walkways and immensely fast escalators.

'The decorative must be abolished.' The problem of *Futurist* architecture must be solved not by plagiarizing China, Persia, or Japan with the aid of photographs, not by foolishly adhering to the rules of Vitruvius, but by strokes of genius and armed with scientific and technical *experience*. Everything must be revolutionary. We must exploit the roofs, utilize the basements, reduce the importance of the façades, transplant the problems of good taste from the petty domain of the section, the capital, the entrance door, to the wider one of great 'groupings of masses', of vast 'town planning projects'. Let us have done with monumental, funereal, commemorative architecture. Let us throw away monuments, sidewalks, arcades, steps; let us sink squares into the ground, raise the level of the city.

I oppose and despise:

1. *All the pseudo avant-garde architecture of Austria, Hungary, Germany, and America.*

2. *All* classical, solemn, hieratic, theatrical, decorative, monumental, frivolous, pleasing architecture.

3. The embalming, reconstruction, and reproduction of monuments *and ancient palaces.*

4. Perpendicular and horizontal lines, cubic and pyramidal forms that are static, heavy, oppressive and absolutely alien to our new sensibility.

And proclaim:

1. That *Futurist* architecture is the architecture of calculation, of audacity and

Antonio Sant'Elia. 1914

simplicity; the architecture of reinforced concrete, of iron, of glass, of pasteboard, of textile fibre, and of all those substitutes for wood, stone, and brick which make possible maximum elasticity and lightness.

2. That this does not render architecture an arid combination of the practical and utilitarian, but that it remains art, that is to say, synthesis and expression.

3. *That oblique and elliptical lines are dynamic by their very nature and have an emotive power a thousand times greater than that of perpendicular and horizontal lines and that a dynamically integrated architecture is impossible without them.*

4. That decoration, as something imposed upon architecture, is an absurdity and that 'the decorative value of *Futurist* architecture depends solely upon the original use and arrangement of the raw or bare or violently coloured material'.

5. That, just as the ancients drew the inspiration for their art from the elements of nature, so we – being materially and spiritually artificial – must find this inspiration in the elements of the immensely new mechanical world which we have created, of which architecture must be the finest expression, the most complete synthesis, the most efficacious artistic integration.

6. *Architecture as the art of arranging the forms of buildings according to pre-determined criteria is finished.*

7. *Architecture must be understood as the endeavour to harmonize, with freedom and great audacity, the environment with man, that is to say, to render the world of things a direct projection of the spirit.*

8. *An architecture so conceived cannot give birth to any three-dimensional or linear habit, because the fundamental characteristics of Futurist architecture will be obsolescence and transience. 'Houses will last less long than we. Each generation will have to build its own city.' This constant renewal of the architectonic environment will contribute to the victory of 'Futurism' already affirmed with 'Words in Freedom', 'Plastic Dynamism', 'Music without Bars', and 'The Art of Sounds', a victory for which we fight without pause against the cowardly worship of the past.*

1918 'De Stijl': Manifesto I

The famous first manifesto of the De Stijl group, the full importance of which can only now be assessed, appeared in November 1918 and introduced the second year of the periodical of the same name. A year earlier a group of radical artists had been formed in Leyden under the leadership of Theo van Doesburg (b.1883 in Utrecht, d.1931 in Davos). Their goal: the organic combination of architecture, sculpture and painting in a lucid, elemental, unsentimental construction. The group took the name 'De Stijl', thereby stating quite precisely that their constructive doctrine was aimed at a new aesthetic. The first word was 'purity'; a 'white' world was to replace the 'brown' one.

1. There is an old and a new consciousness of the age. The old one is directed towards the individual. The new one is directed towards the universal. The struggle of the individual against the universal may be seen both in the world war and in modern art.

2. The war is destroying the old world with its content: individual predominance in every field.

3. The new art has brought to light that which is contained in the new consciousness of the age: a relationship of equality between the universal and the individual.

4. The new consciousness of the age is prepared to realize itself in everything, including external life.

5. Tradition, dogmas and the predominance of the individual stand in the way of this realization.

6. Therefore the founders of the new culture call upon all who believe in reform of art and culture to destroy these obstacles to development, just as in the plastic arts – by doing away with natural form – they have eliminated that which stood in the way of pure artistic expression, the logical conclusion of every artistic concept.

7. The artists of today, all over the world, impelled by one and the same consciousness, have taken part on the spiritual plane in the world war against the domination of individualism, of arbitrariness. They therefore sympathize with all who are fighting spiritually or materially for the formation of an international unity in life, art, and culture.

8. The organ *De Stijl*, founded for this purpose, seeks to contribute towards

setting the new conception of life in a clear light. The collaboration of all is possible by:

Sending in (to the editorial board) as a proof of agreement the (exact) name, address, and profession.

Contributions in the broadest sense (critical, philosophical, architectural, scientific, literary, musical, etc., as well as reproductions) to the monthly magazine *De Stijl*.

Translation into other languages and propagation of the views published in *De Stijl*.

Signatures of the contributors:

Theo van Doesburg, painter | Robt. van't Hoff, architect | Vilmos Huszar, painter | Antony Kok, poet | Piet Mondrian, painter | G. Vantongerloo, sculptor | Jan Wils, architect.

1918 Bruno Taut:
A programme for architecture

Bruno Taut's *Architektur-Programm* (Programme for Architecture) was printed at Christmas 1918 as a leaflet with the approval of the Arbeitsrat für Kunst. This Work Council for Art, with its headquarters in Berlin, was founded at the same time and in close connexion with the November Group, in which the revolutionary artists from all over Germany were gathered together after the war. Unlike the November Group, however, the initiative for the Arbeitsrat rested with a circle of young architects who together with Bruno Taut (b.1880 in Königsberg, d.1938 in Ankara) proclaimed building to be a humanitarian undertaking, a task which Taut summed up in the slogan: 'The earth a good habitation!'

Art – that is one single thing, when it exists! Today there is no art. The various disrupted tendencies can find their way back to a single unity only under the wings of a new architecture, so that every individual discipline will play its part in building. Then there will be no frontiers between the applied arts and sculpture or painting. Everything will be one thing: architecture.

The direct carrier of the spiritual forces, moulder of the sensibilities of the general public, which today are slumbering and tomorrow will awake, is architecture. Only a complete revolution in the spiritual realm will create this architecture. But this revolution, this architecture will not come of themselves. Both must be willed – today's architects must prepare the way for tomorrow's buildings. Their work on the future must receive public assistance to make it possible.

Therefore:

I. Support and gathering together of the ideal forces among architects
(a) Support for architectural ideas which, above and beyond the purely formal aspect, strive for the concentration of all the national energies in the symbol of the building belonging to a better future and which demonstrate the cosmic character of architecture, its religious foundations, so-called Utopias. The provision of public funds in the form of grants to radically inclined architects to enable them to carry out such projects. Financial assistance towards the publication of written material, the construction of models and
(b) for a well-situated experimental site (e.g. in Berlin: the Tempelhofer Feld), on which architects can erect large-scale models of their ideas. Here, too, new architectural effects, e.g. glass as a building material, shall be tried out, perfected and exhibited to the masses in full-scale temporary constructions or individual parts of a building. The layman, the woman, and the child will lead the architect farther than the inhibited specialist. Expenses could be met by melting down public monuments, breaking down triumphal avenues, etc., as well as by the participation of industries connected with the

experimental buildings. Workshops with colonies of craftsmen and artists on the experimental site.

(c) Decision on the distribution of financial aid by a council made up half of creative architects, half of radically minded laymen. If agreement cannot be reached, the final decision will be taken by a layman chosen from the council.

II. People's houses

(a) Beginning of large-scale people's housing estates not inside the towns, but in the open country in connexion with settlements, groups of buildings for theatre and music with lodging houses and the like, culminating in the religious building. Prospect of a prolonged period of construction, hence the beginning should be made according to a grandiose plan with limited means.

(b) Architects to be chosen not by competition but in accordance with I(c).

(c) If building is halted it should be given new incentives during the pauses by means of planned extensions and new ideas in accordance with I(a)–(c).

These buildings should be the first attempt at unifying the energies of the people and of artists, the preliminaries for developing a culture. They cannot stand in the metropolis because the latter, being rotten in itself, will disappear along with the old power. The future lies on the newly developed land, which will feed itself (not 'on the water').

III. Estates

(a) Unitary direction in the sense that one architect will establish overall principles according to which he will examine all projects and buildings, without thereby impeding personal freedom. This architect to have the right of veto.

(b) As II(b).

(c) Formal elements to be reduced radically to second place after agricultural and practical considerations. No fear of extreme simplicity, but also not of colour.

IV. Other buildings

(a) For street development and, according to circumstances, for whole urban districts the same thing applies as for III(a) and (b).

(b) No distinction between public and private buildings. As long as there are freelance architects there will be *only* freelance architects. Until there are State potters there need not be State architects. Public and private buildings may be built by anyone; commissions in line with I(c) or through competitions that are not anonymous, whose participants are invited by a council in accordance with I(c) and awarded prizes; no unpaid designs. Unknown architects will apply for invitation to the council. Anonymity is rendered valueless by the recognizable artistic handwriting of successful architects. No majority decisions by the jury; in the event of no unanimity, each member of the jury is individually responsible for his vote. Best of all a single adjudicator. Final selection possibly by plebiscite.

(c) Building officials, such as municipal building advisers and the like, to be concerned only with the control of local building, demolition, and financial supervision, with purely technical functions. The intermediate fields, such as town planning, to be under the supervision of an advisory council of architects and gardeners.

(d) *No* titles and dignities for architects (doctor, professor, councillor, excellency, etc.)

(e) In everything, preference to be given to the creative; no control over the architect once he has been commissioned.

(f) In the event of public contradiction, decision by a council in accordance with I(c) which can be established by an architects' corporation.

(g) Only such architects' corporations are to have authority in this and other matters and are to be recognized by the State. These corporations are to exercise to the limit the principle of *mutual aid*. They are to bring their influence to bear on the police responsible for enforcing building regulations. Mutual aid alone makes an association fruitful and active. It is more important than the number of votes, which means nothing without social concord. It excludes inartistic and hence unfair competition.

V. The education of architects

(a) Corporations in accordance with IV(g) have the decision as to the building, constitution, and supervision of technical schools; teachers to be selected in collaboration with the students. Practical work on the building site and in the workshop like an apprentice in a craft.

(b) In the trade schools no artistic, but only technical tuition. Technical primary schools.

(c) The artistic education in the offices of practising architects, according to the choice of the young people and the architects themselves.

(d) General education according to inclination and previous knowledge in people's colleges and universities.

VI. Architecture and the other arts

(a) Designing of exhibitions by architects in cheerful shapes; lightweight buildings in busy public squares and parks, on popular lines, almost like a fair.

(b) Extensive employment of painters and sculptors on all buildings in order to draw them away from salon art; the arousal of mutual interest between architect and 'artist'.

(c) In accordance with this principle, also introduction of architectural students into the creative 'new arts'. That architect is alone significant who has a conspectus of the whole domain of art and understands the radical endeavours of painting and sculpture. He alone will help to bring about the unity of the whole.

Increased importance of the architect in public life through his holding important posts and the like will result automatically from the implementation of this programme.

1919 'Work Council for Art':
Under the wing of a great architecture

In March 1919 the Arbeitsrat für Kunst (Work Council for Art) in Berlin published a programmatic circular in which Bruno Taut's *Architektur-Programm* (Programme for Architecture) of 1918 is compressed into a guiding principle and six demands. The Arbeitsrat was then directed by Walter Gropius, César Klein, and Adolf Behne. The business committee included: Otto Bartning, Hermann Hasler, Erich Heckel, Georg Kolbe, Gerhard Marcks, Ludwig Meidner, Max Pechstein, Hermann Richter-Berlin, Karl Schmitt-Rottluff, Bruno Taut, Max Taut, Wilhelm Valentiner. Although the architects were already in the minority, they still had the decisive voice and exercised inner leadership of the group.

In the conviction that the political revolution must be used to liberate art from decades of regimentation, a group of artists and art-lovers united by a common outlook has been formed in Berlin. It strives for the gathering together of all scattered and divided energies which, over and above the protection of one-sided professional interests, wish to work resolutely together for the rebuilding of our whole artistic life. In close contact with associations with similar objectives in other parts of Germany, the Arbeitsrat für Kunst hopes in the not too distant future to be able to push through its aims, which are outlined in the following programme.

In the forefront stands the guiding principle:

Art and people must form a unity.

Art shall no longer be the enjoyment of the few but the life and

happiness of the masses.

The aim is alliance of the arts under the wing of a great architecture.

On this basis six preliminary demands are made:

1. Recognition of the public character of all building activity, both State and private. Removal of all privileges accorded to Civil Servants. Unitary supervision of whole urban districts, streets, and residential estates, without curtailment of freedom over detail. New tasks: people's housing as a means of bringing all the arts to the people. Permanent experimental sites for testing and perfecting new architectural effects.

2. Dissolution of the Academy of Arts, the Academy of Building and the Prussian Provincial Art Commission in their existing form. Replacement of

imagination, unconcerned about technical difficulties. The boon of imagination is always more important than all technique, which always adapts itself to man's creative will. There *are* no architects today, we are all of us merely preparing the way for him who will once again deserve the name of architect, for that means: *lord of art*, who will build gardens out of deserts and pile up wonders to the sky.

Walter Gropius

Is there any architecture today? Are there any architects? Erwin von Steinbach, Sinan, Aben Cencid, Diwakara, Pöppelmann – confronted by these illustrious names, does anyone today dare call himself an 'architect'? No, today there are neither architecture nor architects.

Are not we, who are at the mercy of all-devouring society, parasites in the fabric of a society that knows no architecture, wants no architecture and therefore needs no architects! For we do not call it architecture to give a pleasant shape to a thousand useful things: dwelling houses, offices, stations, markets, schools, water towers, gasometers, fire-stations, factories, and the like. Our 'utility' in these matters, by means of which we earn our living, has nothing to do with our profession, any more than any modern building has anything in common with Angkor Wat, the Alhambra, or the Dresden Zwinger.

In our profession we cannot be creators today, but we are seekers and callers. We shall not cease seeking for that which later may crystallize out, and calling for companions who will go with us on the hard path, who know in deep humility that everything today is nothing but the very first light of dawn, and who prepare themselves in self-forgetful surrender for the rising of the new sun. We call upon all those who believe in the future. All strong longing for the future is architecture in the making. One day there will be a world-view, and then there will also be its sign, its crystal – architecture.

Then there will be no striving, no obsessive seeking for art in the life of various banalities, then there will be one single art, and this art will shine into every nook and cranny. Until then the utilitarian can be tolerable only if the architect bears within him a presentiment of this sun. It alone provides the measure of all things, strictly distinguishes the sacred from the secular, the great from the small, but it also lends to everyday things a shimmer of its radiance.

Bruno Taut

The sketches and designs assembled in this exhibition are for sale. Thus the public have the opportunity to translate their interest in the future destiny of a new architecture, and hence a new art, into deeds by giving material support to the artists by purchasing their sketches, thereby encouraging them to go on working along paths previously blocked by the indifference of the public and the professional simple-mindedness of artists.

We do not expect the snob to buy architectural sketches! The snob is looking for a sensation, an effect. We are hoping for people who have a more responsible conception of their relationship to art. Such helpful purchasers, helpful to the cause and thereby to the artist at the same time, will find a deeper, more lasting joy in the architectural sketches than in many sheets of free drawings. For architectural sketches always stimulate anew the imagination that works with them, builds with them, joins its will to theirs.

To a far higher degree than free graphic works, architectural sketches address themselves to the *will* and thereby fulfil a mission. For we must at all costs escape from the situation in which art lovers are will-less, passive consumers of art.

That the interested public and that the purchasers at our exhibitions are quite different from those who till now have appeared as buyers in the salons is quite certain.

There is nothing small at stake, as Walter Gropius and Bruno Taut have stated here. This exhibition is a first endeavour. Others are to follow – also by unknown painters – new-style exhibitions that break with the exclusive character of exhibitions up to now.

Adolf Behne

1919 Walter Gropius: Programme of the Staatliches Bauhaus in Weimar

The day on which Gropius took over in Weimar from Henry van de Velde (who had to give up his post in 1914 at the beginning of the war) was also the date of the founding of the Staatliches Bauhaus. The renaming of the school was confirmed on 12 April 1919. The same month Gropius (b. 1883 in Berlin, d. 1969 in Boston, Massachusetts) published the founding manifesto and a detailed programme in the shape of a four-page leaflet. The frontispiece (reproduced on page 51) is a woodcut by Lyonel Feininger.

The ultimate aim of all visual arts is the complete building! To embellish buildings was once the noblest function of the fine arts; they were the indispensable components of great architecture. Today the arts exist in isolation, from which they can be rescued only through the conscious, co-operative effort of all craftsmen. Architects, painters, and sculptors must recognize anew and learn to grasp the composite character of a building both as an entity and in its separate parts. Only then will their work be imbued with the architectonic spirit which it has lost as 'salon art'.

The old schools of art were unable to produce this unity; how could they, since art cannot be taught. They must be merged once more with the workshop. The mere drawing and painting world of the pattern designer and the applied artist must become a world that builds again. When young people who take a joy in artistic creation once more begin their life's work by learning a trade, then the unproductive 'artist' will no longer be condemned to deficient artistry, for their skill will now be preserved for the crafts, in which they will be able to achieve excellence.

Architects, sculptors, painters, we all must return to the crafts! For art is not a 'profession'. There is no essential difference between the artist and the craftsman. The artist is an exalted craftsman. In rare moments of inspiration, transcending the consciousness of his will, the grace of heaven may cause his work to blossom into art. But proficiency in a craft is essential to every artist. Therein lies the prime source of creative imagination. Let us then create a new guild of craftsmen without the class distinctions that raise an arrogant barrier between craftsman and artist! Together let us desire, conceive, and create the new structure of the future, which will embrace architecture and sculpture and painting in one unity and which will one day rise toward heaven from the hands of a million workers like the crystal symbol of a new faith.

Walter Gropius

Programme of the Staatliches Bauhaus in Weimar
The Staatliches Bauhaus resulted from the merger of the former Grand-Ducal

Saxon Academy of Art with the former Grand-Ducal Saxon School of Arts and Crafts in conjunction with a newly affiliated department of architecture.

Aims of the Bauhaus

The Bauhaus strives to bring together all creative effort into one whole, to reunify all the disciplines of practical art – sculpture, painting, handicrafts, and the crafts – as inseparable components of a new architecture. The ultimate, if distant, aim of the Bauhaus is the unified work of art – the great structure – in which there is no distinction between monumental and decorative art.

The Bauhaus wants to educate architects, painters, and sculptors of all levels, according to their capabilities, to become competent craftsmen or independent creative artists and to form a working community of leading and future artist-craftsmen. These men, of kindred spirit, will know how to design buildings harmoniously in their entirety – structure, finishing, ornamentation, and furnishing.

Principles of the Bauhaus

Art rises above all methods; in itself it cannot be taught, but the crafts certainly can be. Architects, painters, and sculptors are craftsmen in the true sense of the word: hence, a thorough training in the crafts, acquired in workshops and on experimental and practical sites, is required of all students as the indispensable basis for all artistic production. Our own workshops are to be gradually built up, and apprenticeship agreements with outside workshops will be concluded.

The school is the servant of the workshop and will one day be absorbed in it. Therefore there will be no teachers or pupils in the Bauhaus but masters, journeymen, and apprentices.

The manner of teaching arises from the character of the workshop:

Organic forms developed from manual skills.
Avoidance of all rigidity; priority of creativity; freedom of individuality, but strict study discipline.
Master and journeyman examinations, according to the Guild Statutes, held before the Council of Masters of the Bauhaus or before outside masters.
Collaboration by the students in the work of the masters.
Securing of commissions, also for students.
Mutual planning of extensive, Utopian structural designs – public buildings and buildings for worship – aimed at the future. Collaboration of all masters and students – architects, painters, sculptors – on these designs with the object of gradually achieving a harmony of all the component elements and parts that make up architecture.
Constant contact with the leaders of the crafts and industries of the country.
Contact with public life, with the people, through exhibitions and other activities.

New research into the nature of the exhibitions, to solve the problem of displaying visual work and sculpture within the framework of architecture. Encouragement of friendly relations between masters and students outside of work; therefore plays, lectures, poetry, music, fancy-dress parties. Establishment of a cheerful ceremonial at these gatherings.

Range of Instruction
Instruction at the Bauhaus includes all practical and scientific areas of creative work.
A. Architecture,
B. Painting,
C. Sculpture
including all branches of the crafts.
Students are trained in a craft (1) as well as in drawing and painting (2) and science and theory (3).

1. Craft training – either in our own, gradually enlarging workshops or in outside workshops to which the student is bound by apprenticeship agreement – includes:
(a) sculptors, stonemasons, stucco workers, woodcarvers, ceramic workers, plaster casters;
(b) blacksmiths, locksmiths, founders, metal turners;
(c) cabinetmakers;
(d) scene-painters, glass painters, mosaic workers, enamellers;
(e) etchers, wood engravers, lithographers, art printers, enchasers;
(f) weavers.
Craft training forms the basis of all teaching at the Bauhaus. Every student must learn a craft.

2. Training in drawing and painting includes:
(a) free-hand sketching from memory and imagination;
(b) drawing and painting of heads, live models, and animals;
(c) drawing and painting of landscapes, figures, plants, and still-lifes;
(d) composition;
(e) execution of murals, panel pictures, and religious shrines;
(f) design of ornaments;
(g) lettering;
(h) construction and projection drawing;
(i) design of exteriors, gardens, and interiors;
(j) design of furniture and practical articles.

3. Training in science and theory includes:
(a) art history – not presented in the sense of a history of styles, but rather to further active understanding of historical working methods and techniques;
(b) science of materials;
(c) anatomy – from the living model;

(d) physical and chemical theory of colour;
(e) rational painting methods;
(f) basic concepts of bookkeeping, contract negotiations, personnel;
(g) individual lectures on subjects of general interest in all areas of art and science.

Divisions of Instruction
The training is divided into three courses of instruction:

  I. course for apprentices;
 II. course for journeymen;
III. course for junior masters.

The instruction of the individual is left to the discretion of each master within the framework of the general programme and the work schedule, which is revised every semester. In order to give the students as versatile and comprehensive a technical and artistic training as possible the work schedule will be so arranged that every architect-, painter-, and sculptor-to-be is able to participate in part of the other courses.

Admission
Any person of good repute, without regard to age or sex, whose previous education is deemed adequate by the Council of Masters will be admitted, as far as space permits. The tuition fee is 180 marks per year (it will gradually disappear entirely with increasing earnings of the Bauhaus). A non-recurring admission fee of 20 marks is also to be paid. Foreign students pay double fees. Address enquiries to the Secretariat of the Staatliches Bauhaus in Weimar.

April 1919.
The Administration of the Staatliches Bauhaus in Weimar:
Walter Gropius

1919   Erich Mendelsohn:
The problem of a new architecture (excerpt)

Erich Mendelsohn (b.1887 in Allenstein, East Prussia, d.1953 in San Francisco) was in 1919 a member of the Central Committee of the November Group. In the leaflet of the Berlin Arbeitsrat für Kunst (p.44) he is listed as one of those friends who have expressed their support for the goals of the Arbeitsrat. The following text is an excerpt from a programmatic lecture with slides which Mendelsohn delivered to members of the Arbeitsrat. The lecture presupposes a knowledge of the Utopian designs assembled by the Arbeitsrat in its exhibition of April 1919. Mendelsohn compares these designs with those buildings already regarded as standard examples of the new development.

The simultaneous process of revolutionary political decisions and radical changes in human relationships in economy and science and religion and art give belief in the new form an *a priori* right to exercise control, and provide a justifiable basis for a rebirth amidst the misery produced by world-historical disasters.

When forms break up, they are merely thrust aside by new forms that are already present but only now come to light.

For the particular prerequisites of architecture, the reorganization of society taking place in response to the spirit of the times means new tasks arising out of the changed purposes of buildings which in turn result from changes in travel, economy, and religion, coupled with new possibilities presented by the new building materials: glass, iron, and concrete.

When we consider as yet unknown possibilities, we must not let ourselves be misled by that dulling of vision which comes from too close a viewpoint. That which seems today to be flowing with viscous slowness will later appear to history as having moved at a breakneck and thrilling speed. We are dealing here with an act of creation!

We are only at the early beginning, but we are already faced with the possibilities of its development.

Before such a future the great achievements of *historical* times step back of their own accord; the immediacy of the *present* loses its importance.

What will happen has value *only* if it comes into being in the intoxication of vision.

Criticism bears fruit *only* if it can embrace the whole problem. Tutelage fails, because the future speaks for itself. If we wish to pass on such a faith, to convey its palpable conclusions to a wider circle as self-evident facts, we must necessarily demonstrate that the young forces in architecture draw their architectonic experiences not from *history* nor from heaven, but solely from the fertility of their own visions of space. In this, up to the present, three paths may be distinguished, which, though fundamentally different, follow parallel courses towards the same goal and nevertheless will one day cross . . .

It cannot be chance that the three recognizable paths of the new architecture coincide with the same number and nature of the new paths in painting and sculpture.

This coincidence of the volition behind them will find expression in the resulting work and will bring all the arts back into a unity. This unity will embrace the great achievements – the shrines of a new world – *as well as* the smallest objects in our everyday dwellings.

What today is a *problem* – will one day be a *task*; what today is the vision and faith of a single individual, will one day become a law for *all*.

Therefore *all* trends seem necessary to achieving the goal, and hence to solving the problem of a new architecture:

the apostles of glass worlds,

the analysts of spatial elements,

the seekers for new forms of material and construction.

Naturally, this era will not be brought into being by social classes in the grip of tradition.

Only a *new* will has the future in its favour in the unconsciousness of its chaotic impetus, in the pristine vigour with which it embraces the universal.

For just as every epoch that was decisive for the evolution of human history united the *whole* known globe under its spiritual will, so what we long for will have to bring happiness beyond our *own* country, beyond Europe, to *all* peoples. This does not mean that I am handing over the reins to internationalism. For *internationalism* means an aesthetic attitude with its basis in no one people in a disintegrating world. *Supra-nationalism*, however, embraces *national* demarcations as a *precondition*; it is free humanity that *alone* can reestablish an all-embracing culture.

Such a great will unites all those who are engaged in the work.

It comes into being, it awakens an adequate religious faith *only* after the fusion of the ultimate achievement of *all* peoples.

Here we can do no *more* than contribute the modest measure of our own work, in faith and in a willingness to serve.

1920 Naum Gabo/Antoine Pevsner: Basic principles of Constructivism

The brothers Gabo and Pevsner, both sculptors, wrote in Moscow in 1920 the *Realist Manifesto*, in which they laid down the basic principles of Constructivism, which exercised a powerful influence especially on post-war Russian architecture (Tatlin, the brothers Vesnin, Lissitzky). Gabo and Pevsner are concerned with constructions in space, which, however, are interpreted primarily not as architecture, but as sculpture. An important part is played in their conceptions by haptic and optic charms arising out of the combination of various materials in these spatial constructions. These materials are without exception those produced industrially.

1. We reject the closed spatial circumference as the plastic expression of the moulding of space. We assert that space can only be modelled from within outward in its depth, not from without inward through its volume. For what else is absolute space than a unique, coherent, and unlimited depth?

2. We reject the closed mass as an exclusive element for the building up of three-dimensional and architectonic bodies in space. In opposition to it we set the demand that plastic bodies shall be constructed stereometrically.

3. We reject decorative colour as a painterly element in three-dimensional construction. We demand that the concrete material shall be employed as a painterly element.

4. We reject the decorative line. We demand of every line in the work of art that it shall serve solely to define the inner directions of force in the body to be portrayed.

5. We are no longer content with the static elements of form in plastic art. We demand the inclusion of time as a new element and assert that real movement must be employed in plastic art, in order to make possible the use of kinetic rhythms in a way that is not merely illusionistic.

1920   Bruno Taut:
Down with seriousism!

In November 1919 the Berlin Arbeitsrat für Kunst was merged with the
November Group. But Taut and Behne kept together their architect friends.
At their instigation there was an exchange of circular letters, sketches, and
essays in the nature of confessions of faith, known as *Die Gläserne Kette* (The
Glass Chain). From January 1920 onward Taut had a new mouthpiece: in every
issue of the periodical *Stadtbaukunst alter und neuer Zeit* (Urban Architecture
Ancient and Modern) he had four to six pages to do with as he liked. Taut called
this appendix *Frühlicht*[1] (Daybreak). The text reproduced below occupies
the introductory page of this series.

Hopp! Hopp! Hopp! My sweet little horsey!
Hopp! Hopp! Hopp! Where do you want to go?
Over that high wall?
Well really I don't know!
Hopp! Hopp! Hopp! My sweet little horsey!
Hopp! Hopp! Hopp! Where – do – you – want – to go?
(Scheerbart, *Katerpoesie*)

Away with the sourpusses, the wailing Willies, the sobersides, the brow
furrowers, the eternally serious, the sweet-sour ones, the forever important!
'Important! Important!' This damned habit of acting important! Tomb-
stone and cemetery façades in front of junk shops and old clothes stores!
Smash the shell-lime Doric, Ionic and Corinthian columns, demolish the pin-
heads! Down with the 'respectability' of sandstone and plate-glass, in frag-
ments with the rubbish of marble and precious wood, to the garbage heap
with all that junk!
'Oh, our concepts: space, home, style!' Ugh, how these concepts stink!
Destroy them, put an end to them! Let nothing remain! Chase away their
schools, let the professorial wigs fly, we'll play catch with them. Blast, blast!
Let the dusty, matted, gummed up world of concepts, ideologies and systems
feel our cold north wind! Death to the concept-lice! Death to everything
stuffy! Death to everything called title, dignity, authority! Down with everything serious!
Down with all camels that won't go through the eye of a needle, with all
worshippers of Mammon and Moloch! 'The worshippers of force must
knuckle under to force!' We are sick of their bloodsucking – caterwauling in
the early light.
In the distance shines our tomorrow. Hurray, three times hurray for our

---

[1] B. TAUT. *Frühlicht – Eine Folge für die Verwirklichung des neuen Baugedankens.* Ullstein,
Bauwelt Fundamente, Vol.8.

kingdom without force! Hurray for the transparent, the clear! Hurray for purity! Hurray for crystal! Hurray and again hurray for the fluid, the graceful, the angular, the sparkling, the flashing, the light – hurray for everlasting architecture!

1920   Le Corbusier:
Towards a new architecture: guiding principles

Le Corbusier (b.1887 in La Chaux-de-Fonds, Switzerland, d.1965 in Roquebrune, Cap-Martin, France) was already well known outside France when in 1920–1 those programmatic notes appeared in the periodical *L'Esprit Nouveau* which in 1923 he published in book form under the title *Vers une Architecture*. In 1910 Le Corbusier had worked for a few months with Peter Behrens in Berlin, knew the work of the Deutscher Werkbund (which, against van de Velde's protest – see page 28 – was already concerning itself with standardization and the problems of industrialization), had since 1917 travelled all over Europe and was now, from 1920, evolving an aesthetic of mass-production building.

The engineer's aesthetic and architecture

The Engineer's Aesthetic and Architecture are two things that march together and follow one from the other: the one being now at its full height, the other in an unhappy state of retrogression.

The Engineer, inspired by the law of Economy and governed by mathematical calculation, puts us in accord with universal law. He achieves harmony.

The Architect, by his arrangement of forms, realizes an order which is a pure creation of his spirit; by forms and shapes he affects our senses to an acute degree and provokes plastic emotions; by the relationships which he creates he wakes profound echoes in us, he gives us the measure of an order which we feel to be in accordance with that of our world, he determines the various movements of our heart and of our understanding; it is then that we experience the sense of beauty.

Three reminders to architects

Mass

Our eyes are constructed to enable us to see forms in light.
Primary forms are beautiful forms because they can be clearly appreciated.
Architects today no longer achieve these simple forms.
Working by calculation, engineers employ geometrical forms, satisfying our eyes by their geometry and our understanding by their mathematics; their work is on the direct line of good art.

Surface

A mass is enveloped in its surface, a surface which is divided up according to the directing and generating lines of the mass; and this gives the mass its individuality.
Architects today are afraid of the geometrical constituents of surfaces.
The great problems of modern construction must have a geometrical solution.
Forced to work in accordance with the strict needs of exactly determined

conditions, engineers make use of form-generating and form-defining elements. They create limpid and moving plastic facts.

Plan
The Plan is the generator.
Without a plan, you have lack of order and wilfulness.
The Plan holds in itself the essence of sensation.
The great problems of tomorrow, dictated by collective necessities, put the question of 'plan' in a new form.
Modern life demands, and is waiting for, a new kind of plan, both for the house and for the city.

Regulating lines
An inevitable element of Architecture.
The necessity for order. The regulating line is a guarantee against wilfulness. It brings satisfaction to the understanding.
The regulating line is a means to an end; it is not a recipe. Its choice and the modalities of expression given to it are an integral part of architectural creation.

Eyes which do not see ...

Liners
A great epoch has begun.
There exists a new spirit.
There exists a mass of work conceived in the new spirit; it is to be met with particularly in industrial production.
Architecture is stifled by custom.
The 'styles' are a lie.
Style is a unity of principle animating all the work of an epoch, the result of a state of mind which has its own special character.
Our own epoch is determining, day by day, its own style.
Our eyes, unhappily, are unable yet to discern it.

Aeroplanes
The aeroplane is the product of close selection.
The lesson of the aeroplane lies in the logic which governed the statement of the problem and its realization.
The problem of the house has not yet been stated.
Nevertheless there do exist standards for the dwelling house.
Machinery contains in itself the factor of economy, which makes for selection.
The house is a machine for living in.

Automobiles
We must aim at the fixing of standards in order to face the problem of perfection.

The Parthenon is a product of selection applied to a standard.

Architecture operates in accordance with standards.

Standards are a matter of logic, analysis, and minute study; they are based on a problem which has been well 'stated'. A standard is definitely established by experiment.

Architecture

The lesson of Rome

The business of Architecture is to establish emotional relationships by means of raw materials.

Architecture goes beyond utilitarian needs.

Architecture is a plastic thing.

The spirit of order, a unity of intention.

The sense of relationships; architecture deals with quantities.

Passion can create drama out of inert stone.

The illusion of plans

The Plan proceeds from within to without; the exterior is the result of an interior.

The elements of architecture are light and shade, walls and space.

Arrangement is the gradation of aims, the classification of intentions.

Man looks at the creation of architecture with his eyes, which are 5 feet 6 inches from the ground. One can only deal with aims which the eye can appreciate, and intentions which take into account architectural elements. If there come into play intentions which do not speak the language of architecture, you arrive at the illusion of plans, you transgress the rules of the Plan through an error in conception, or through a leaning towards empty show.

Pure creation of the mind

Contour and profile are the touchstone of the architect.

Here he reveals himself as artist or mere engineer.

Contour is free of all constraint.

There is here no longer any question of custom, nor of tradition, nor of construction nor of adaptation to utilitarian needs.

Contour and profile are a pure creation of the mind; they call for the plastic artist.

Mass-production houses

A great epoch has begun.

There exists a new spirit.

Industry, overwhelming us like a flood which rolls on towards its destined ends, has furnished us with new tools adapted to this new epoch, animated by the new spirit.

Economic law inevitably governs our acts and our thoughts.

The problem of the house is a problem of the epoch. The equilibrium of society today depends upon it. Architecture has for its first duty, in this period of renewal, that of bringing about a revision of values, a revision of the constituent elements of the house.

Mass-production is based on analysis and experiment.

Industry on the grand scale must occupy itself with building and establish the elements of the house on a mass-production basis.

We must create the mass-production spirit.

The spirit of constructing mass-production houses.

The spirit of living in mass-production houses.

The spirit of conceiving mass-production houses.

If we eliminate from our hearts and minds all dead concepts in regard to the house, and look at the question from a critical and objective point of view, we shall arrive at the 'House-Machine', the mass-production house, healthy (and morally so too) and beautiful in the same way that the working tools and instruments which accompany our existence are beautiful.

Beautiful also with all the animation that the artist's sensibility can add to severe and pure functioning elements.

Architecture or revolution (excerpt)

... In building and construction, mass-production has already been begun; in face of new economic needs, mass-production units have been created both in mass and detail; and definite results have been achieved both in detail and in mass. If this fact be set against the past, then you have revolution, both in the method employed and in the large scale on which it has been carried out.

... Our minds have consciously or unconsciously apprehended these events and new needs have arisen, consciously or unconsciously.

The machinery of Society, profoundly *out of gear*, oscillates between an amelioration, of historical importance, and a catastrophe.

The primordial instinct of every human being is to assure himself of a shelter. The various classes of workers in society today *no longer have dwellings adapted to their needs; neither the artisan nor the intellectual.*

It is a question of building which is at the root of the social unrest of today: architecture or revolution.

1921　Bruno Taut:
Frühlicht (Daybreak)

In July 1920 Bruno Taut had to end the first series of his *Frühlicht* articles. The editor of *Stadtbaukunst* considered these contributions no longer tolerable. In 1921 Taut went as municipal architect to Magdeburg and from there, from autumn 1921 on, he was able to continue the publication as a quarterly periodical. Once again the friends of The Glass Chain had a chance to speak. Once again Taut prefaced the first publication with a piece of expressive, hymn-like prose. But in the ensuing issues it became clear that new ideas and forces were finding expression, new ideas and forces more closely related to reality. And new names: Oud, Mächler, Mies van der Rohe.

HOW DAY WILL EVENTUALLY BREAK – WHO KNOWS? BUT WE CAN FEEL THE MORNING. WE ARE NO LONGER MOONSTRUCK WANDERERS ROAMING DREAMILY IN THE PALE LIGHT OF HISTORY. A COOL EARLY MORNING WIND IS BLOWING AROUND US; HE WHO DOESN'T WANT TO SHIVER MUST STRIDE OUT. AND WE AND ALL THOSE STRIDING WITH US SEE IN THE DISTANCE THE EARLY LIGHT OF THE AWAKENING MORNING! WHERE ARE ALL THE NOCTURNAL SPECTRES! GLASSY AND BRIGHT A NEW WORLD SHINES OUT IN THE EARLY LIGHT, IT IS SENDING OUT ITS FIRST RAYS. A FIRST GLEAM OF JUBILANT DAWN. DECADES, GENERATIONS – AND THE GREAT SUN OF ARCHITECTURE, OF ART IN GENERAL WILL BEGIN ITS VICTORIOUS COURSE. / THE IDEA OF THE EARLY LIGHT IS NOT MIRRORED IN THIS SERIES FOR THE FIRST TIME. IT WAS AND IS GOOD TO MAINTAIN OUR VIEW OF THE HORIZON WITH UNDIMMED IMAGINATION. TESTS OF THE REALIZATION OF THE NEW IDEA ALREADY EXIST IN MATERIAL, AND THESE PAGES ARE INTENDED FIRST AND FOREMOST TO SERVE THIS REALIZATION, STARTING FROM THE ACTIVITIES OF A TOWN COUNCIL THAT DELIGHTS IN THE FUTURE. THEY ARE INTENDED TO HELP OUR COMRADES IN GERMANY STRIDE FORWARD MORE JOYFULLY WITH US, AND OUR PATHS WILL MEET THOSE WHO ARE OUR BROTHERS IN SPIRIT BEYOND OUR FRONTIERS. / WE DO NOT BELIEVE IN PARALLELS BETWEEN MATERIAL AND SPIRITUAL FLOWERING. THE FULL STOMACH DOES NOT LIKE IDEAS, THE OVERFULL HATES THEM, IT WANTS PEACE. TODAY MORE THAN EVER WE BELIEVE IN OUR WILL, WHICH CREATES FOR US THE ONLY LIFE VALUE. AND THIS VALUE IS: EVERLASTING CHANGE.

1922 'De Stijl': Creative demands

De Stijl made its voice heard all over Europe. Month by month the periodical spread the principles of elemental creativity. Theo van Doesburg travelled from city to city delivering lectures. 'The progressive architects of Holland have adopted an international standpoint.' Which 'has grown up out of practice'. The field of practice had itself expanded. In 1920 *De Stijl* formulated its literature manifesto and in 1921 the manifesto *Vers une nouvelle formation du monde*. At the International Artists Congress in Düsseldorf in May 1922 van Doesburg announced: 'We are preparing the way for the use of an objective universal means of creation.'

1. The end of exhibitions. Instead: demonstration rooms for total works.

2. An international exchange of ideas concerning creative problems.

3. The development of a universal means of creation for all arts.

4. An end to the division between art and life. (Art becomes life.)

5. An end to the division between artist and man.

Theo van Doesburg, 1922

1923 'De Stijl':
Manifesto V: − □ + = R₄

'Towards Collective Building' is the heading over *De Stijl Manifesto V*, written in Paris. Collective building means: constructive collaboration of architect, sculptor, and painter in a work existing in space and time. All work to be carried out according to the elemental laws of the specific material. The result of this work will be a flawless unity of the arts, from which all individual emotions have been banished. In *De Stijl VI* Theo van Doesburg and Cor van Eesteren comment on the Paris manifesto: art and life can no longer be separated. Hence the term art has become unusable. We are seeking an objective system.

I. In close co-operation we have examined architecture as a plastic unit made up of industry and technology and have established that a new style has emerged as a result.

II. We have examined the laws of space and their endless variations (i.e. spatial contrasts, spatial dissonances, spatial supplementations) and have established that all these variations can be welded together into a balanced unity.

III. We have examined the laws of colour in space and time and have established that the mutual harmonization of these elements produces a new and positive unity.

IV. We have examined the relationships between space and time and found that the process of rendering these two elements visible through the use of colour produces a new dimension.

V. We have examined the mutual interrelationships between dimension, proportion, space, time and material and have discovered a final method of constructing a unity from them.

VI. By breaking up enclosing elements (walls, etc.) we have eliminated the duality of interior and exterior.

VII. We have given colour its rightful place in architecture and we assert that painting separated from the architectonic construction (i.e. the picture) has no right to exist.

VIII. The time of destruction is at an end. A new age is dawning: the age of construction.

van Eesteren | Theo van Doesburg | G. Rietveld

Van Doesburg and van Eesteren:
Towards collective building

Commentary on Manifesto V

We have to realize that art and life are no longer separate domains. Therefore the idea of 'art' as illusion unconnected with real life has to disappear. The word 'art' no longer means anything to us. Leaving this concept behind us, we demand the construction of our environment according to creative laws derived from a fixed principle. These laws, linked with those of economics, mathematics, technology, hygiene, etc., lead to a new plastic unity. In order that the interrelationships of these reciprocal laws may be defined, the laws themselves must first be established and understood. Up to now the field of human creativity and the laws governing its constructions have never been examined scientifically.

These laws cannot be imagined. They exist as facts and can be elucidated only by collective work and by experience.

Our era is inimical to all subjective speculation in art, science, technology, and so on. The new spirit which already governs almost all modern life is opposed to animal spontaneity (lyricism), to the dominion of nature, to complicated hair-styles and elaborate cooking.

In order to create something new we need a method, that is to say, an objective system. If we discover the same qualities in different things, we have found an objective scale. For example, one of the basic laws is that the modern constructor, by the means proper to his particular field of activity, brings to light not the relationship between things themselves, but the relationship between their qualities.

Oskar Schlemmer, 1922

1923   Oskar Schlemmer:
Manifesto for the first Bauhaus exhibition

Although this manifesto in the publicity leaflet for the first Bauhaus exhibition
in Weimar (July to September 1923) was written with the approval in principle
of Oskar Schlemmer's board of governors, it went to press before the board had
been able to look at the text. Because of the statement that the Bauhaus was a
gathering point for those who wished to build the 'cathedral of Socialism' the
manifesto section of the leaflet was pulped. The precaution was in vain. Several
complete copies reached the public and brought the Bauhaus under suspicion of
being an institution that dabbled in politics.

The Staatliches Bauhaus in Weimar is the first and so far the only government
school in the Reich – if not in the world – which calls upon the creative forces
of the fine arts to become influential while they are vital. At the same time it
endeavours, through the establishment of workshops founded upon the
crafts, to unite and productively stimulate the arts with the aim of combining
them in architecture. The concept of building will restore the unity that
perished in debased academicism and in finicky handicraft. It must reinstate
the broad relationship with the 'whole' and, in the deepest sense, make
possible the total work of art. The ideal is old, but its rendering always new:
the fulfilment is the style, and never was the 'will-to-style' more powerful than
today. But confusion about concepts and attitudes caused the conflict and
dispute over the nature of this style which will emerge as the 'new beauty'
from the clash of ideas. Such a school, animating and inwardly animated,
unintentionally becomes the gauge for the convulsions of the political and
intellectual life of the time, and the history of the Bauhaus becomes the
history of contemporary art.

The Staatliches Bauhaus, founded after the catastrophe of the war in the
chaos of the revolution and in the era of the flowering of an emotion-laden,
explosive art, becomes the rallying-point of all those who, with belief in the
future and with sky-storming enthusiasm, wish to build the 'cathedral of
Socialism'. The triumphs of industry and technology before the war and the
orgies in the name of destruction during it called to life that impassioned
romanticism which was a flaming protest against materialism and the mechanization of art and life. The misery of the time was also a spiritual anguish. A
cult of the unconscious and of the unexplainable, a propensity for mysticism
and sectarianism, originated in the quest for those highest things which are in
danger of being deprived of their meaning in a world full of doubt and dis-
ruption. Breaking the limitations of classical aesthetics reinforced boundless-
ness of feeling, which found nourishment and verification in the discovery of the
East and the art of the Negro, peasants, children, and the insane. The origin
of artistic creation was as much sought after as its limits were courageously
extended. Passionate use of the means of expression developed in altar paintings. But it is in pictures, and always in pictures, where the decisive values take

refuge. As the highest achievement of individual exaggeration, free from bonds and unredeemed, they must all, apart from the unity of the picture itself, remain in debt to the proclaimed synthesis. The honest crafts wallowed in the exotic joy of materials, and architecture piled Utopian schemes on paper.

Reversal of values, changes in point of view, name and concept, result in the other view, the next faith. Dada, court jester in this kingdom, plays ball with paradoxes and makes the atmosphere free and easy. Americanisms transferred to Europe, the new wedged into the old world, death to the past, to moonlight, and to the soul, thus the present time strides along with the gestures of a conqueror. Reason and science, 'man's greatest powers', are the regents, and the engineer is the sedate executor of unlimited possibilities. Mathematics, structure, and mechanization are the elements, and power and money are the dictators of these modern phenomena of steel, concrete, glass, and electricity. Velocity of rigid matter, dematerialization of matter, organization of inorganic matter, all these produce the miracle of abstraction. Based on the laws of nature, these are the achievements of mind in the conquest of nature, based on the power of capital, the work of man against man. The speed and supertension of commercialism make expediency and utility the measure of all effectiveness, and calculation seizes the transcendent world: art becomes a logarithm. Art, long bereft of its name, lives a life after death, in the monument of the cube and in the coloured square. Religion is the precise process of thinking, and God is dead. Man, self-conscious and perfect being, surpassed in accuracy by every puppet, awaits results from the chemist's retort until the formula for 'spirit' is found as well . . .

Goethe: 'If the hopes materialize that men, with all their strength, with heart and mind, with understanding and love, will join together and become conscious of each other, then what no man can yet imagine will occur – Allah will no longer need to create, we will create his world.' This is the synthesis, the concentration, intensification, and compression of all that is positive to form the powerful mean. The idea of the mean, far from mediocrity and weakness, taken as scale and balance, becomes the idea of German art.

Germany, country of the middle, and Weimar, the heart of it, is not for the first time the adopted place of intellectual decision. What matters is the recognition of what is pertinent to us, so that we will not aimlessly wander astray. In balancing the polar contrasts – loving the remotest past as well as the remotest future; averting reaction as much as anarchism; advancing from the end-in-itself and from self-directedness to the typical, from the problematical to the valid and secure – we become the bearers of responsibility and the conscience of the world. An idealism of activity that embraces, penetrates, and unites art, science, and technology and that influences research, study, and work will construct the 'art-edifice' of Man, which is but an allegory of the cosmic system. Today we can do no more than ponder the total plan, lay the foundations, and prepare the building stones.

But

We exist! We have the will! We are producing!

1923 Werner Graeff:
The new engineer is coming

The first number of the periodical *G – Material zur elementaren Gestaltung* (material for elemental creativity) – appeared in July 1923 in Berlin. The publisher was the film pioneer Hans Richter; his fellow editors were Werner Graeff (b.1901 in Wuppertal, lives in Essen) and El Lissitzky (b.1890 in Smolensk, d.1941 in Moscow). The editorial programme followed in its essential points the principles of the Stijl group. A new concept was introduced: 'The basic requirement for the creation of elemental form is *economy*. A pure relationship between force and material. This calls for elemental means, complete mastery of the means. Elemental order, adherence to laws.' Werner Graeff's contribution is dated December 1922. Alongside it stand theses from the *Realist Manifesto*, Moscow 1920.

Essential criterion for modern, creative people:
The capacity to think and fashion elementally.
The school for the new creation of form is: to elucidate the elements of every creative domain radically and unimpeachably. And: to live the modern world-view in its most extreme implications.
Now the new generation of engineers is growing up!
This means: first the perfection – then the end of mechanistic technology. The last mighty soaring of mechanistic technology, because the requisite laws are a component of the modern world-view that has been *mastered* and the means for the creation of elemental form are *perfectly clear* to the new engineer.
Necessary consequences of this clarity and mastery are: simplicity, balance, naturalness, the shrewdest economy.
The new engineer does not modify, he creates afresh; that is to say, he does not improve, but provides an *absolutely elemental* fulfilment of every demand.
In a few years, the new elementally trained generation of engineers will easily fulfil every demand that can rationally be made upon mechanistic technology.
BUT THIS IS NOT THE END:
Above and beyond this, an immense, far more magnificent field, whose first outlines are already emerging in science and art, will open up to the leaders among the new creators. In a decade hypotheses will develop into theories – and finally into mastered *laws*. Then the capacity to treat every fresh demand in an absolutely elemental manner will lead forward only when it has become part of man's flesh and blood.
The new, more splendid technology of tensions, of invisible movements, of remote control and speeds such as cannot even be imagined in 1922 will come into being, uninfluenced by the methods of mechanistic technology.
The new engineer is ready and waiting. *Long live elemental creativity!*

1923 Erich Mendelsohn: Dynamics and function (excerpt)

> After his exhibition at Cassirer's in 1919 Mendelsohn was invited to contribute to the Amsterdam periodical *Wendingen*. An issue devoted to his work appeared in October 1920. This brought Mendelsohn into close contact with the group of architects calling themselves Architectura et Amicitia in Amsterdam (to whom he delivered the lecture 'Dynamics and Function' in 1923); but he also got to know their opponents, J. J. P. Oud and members of the Rotterdam De Stijl group. As early as 1919 Mendelsohn wrote to his wife: 'The two groups must find their way to one another . . . Otherwise Rotterdam will construct itself into a cool death, Amsterdam will dynamize itself into the magic of a conflagration . . . Functional dynamism is the postulate.'

Ever since science has come to realize that the two concepts matter and energy, formerly kept rigidly apart, are merely different states of the same primary element, that in the order of the world nothing takes place without relativity to the cosmos, without relationship to the whole, the engineer has abandoned the mechanical theory of dead matter and has reaffirmed his allegiance to nature. From primal states he deduces the laws determining interactions. His former arrogance has given way to the happy sense of being a creator. The intellectually *one-sided* inventor has become the intuitive *many-sided* originator. The machine, till now the pliable tool of lifeless exploitation, has become the constructive element of a new, living organism. We owe its existence neither to the whim of an unknown donor nor to the joy in invention of a constructive genius; it comes into being as a necessary concomitant of evolution at the *same* moment as need demands it. Its real task lies in satisfying the multiple mutual interrelationships between population figures and increased production, between industrialization and human consumption; it has to bring order into these interrelationships and master their effects.

Thus it becomes both a symbol of intensified decay and an element in a life that is ordering itself anew.

Now that we have discovered its forces we apparently *dominate* nature. In reality we merely serve it with new means.

We have apparently freed ourselves from the law of gravity.

In truth we merely comprehend its logic with new senses. The precision of its revolutions, the harsh sound of its course, impel us to fresh clarity, the metallic gleam of its material thrusts us into a fresh light.

A new rhythm is taking possession of the world, a new movement.

Medieval man, amidst the horizontal tranquillity of his contemplative working day, needed the verticals of the cathedrals in order to find his God high above. Modern man, amidst the excited flurry of his fast-moving life, can find equilibrium only in the tension-free horizontal. Only by means of his will to reality can he become master of his unrest, only by moving at maximum speed will he overcome his haste. For the rotating earth stands still! It is unthinkable that mastery of the air, dominion over the natural elements should be given up.

The task is to reduce them to commonplaces of knowledge.

The child learns to telephone; numbers have lost their magnitude; distances have been reduced to short walks.

Technology is handicraft. The laboratory is a workplace. The inventor is master.

... Rarely, it seems to me, has the order of the world so unequivocally revealed itself; rarely has the Logos of existence opened wider than in this time of supposed chaos. For we have all been shaken awake by elemental events; we have had time to shake off prejudices and sated complacency. As creators ourselves we know how very variously the forces of motion, the play of tensions, work out in individual instances. All the more, then, is it our task to oppose excited flurry with contemplation, exaggeration with simplicity, uncertainty with a clear law; to rediscover the elements of energy in the midst of the fragmentation of energy, from the elements of energy to form a new whole. To work, construct, re-calculate the Earth! But *form* the world that is waiting for you. Form with the dynamics of your blood the functions of its reality, elevate its functions to dynamic supra-sensuality. Simple and certain as the machine, clear and bold as construction. From real presuppositions form art, from mass and light form intangible space. But do not forget that the individual creation can be understood only within the context of the totality of the phenomena of the age. It is just as bound to the relativity of its facts as present and future are to the relativity of history.

1923 Ludwig Mies van der Rohe: Working theses

Mies van der Rohe's theses, written in May 1923, appeared together with his design for an office building of reinforced concrete (1922) in the first number of G, of which Mies was one of the founders. Apart from Mies (b. 1886 in Aix-la-Chapelle, d. 1969 in Chicago), Graeff, and Richter, other contributors were Gabo, Pevsner, Haussmann – all of whom were living in Berlin at the time – and Doesburg in Paris. This was a surprising concentration and meeting of forces: De Stijl and Russian Constructivism met at a place at which, just half a year earlier, in winter 1922–3 on the occasion of the architectural exhibition in the Berlin Secession, critics had unanimously stated: this is the 'New Architecture'.

We reject { all aesthetic speculation, all doctrine, and all formalism.

Architecture is the will of the age conceived in spatial terms.

Living. Changing. New.

Not yesterday, not tomorrow, only today can be given form.

Only this architecture creates.

Create form out of the nature of the task with the means of our time.

This is our work.

O F F I C E B U I L D I N G

The office building is a house of work of organization of clarity of economy.

Bright, wide workrooms, easy to oversee, undivided except as the organism of the undertaking is divided. The maximum effect with the minimum expenditure of means.

The materials are concrete iron glass.

74

Reinforced concrete buildings are by nature skeletal buildings. No noodles nor armoured turrets. A construction of girders that carry the weight, and walls that carry no weight. That is to say, buildings consisting of skin and bones.

1923 Arthur Korn:
Analytical and Utopian architecture

This programmatic essay appeared in December 1923 in Paul Westheim's
Kunstblatt. Arthur Korn (b.1891 in Breslau, lives in London) was in 1919 a
partner with Mendelsohn and in 1922 opened an office with Sigfried
Weitzmann. Apart from interior designs and dwelling houses in Berlin and
Silesia, Korn did a great deal of work for Jerusalem and Haifa. In 1923 he
designed a business centre for Haifa that won second prize in the competition
and was included by Gropius in Volume One of the Bauhaus books
(*Internationale Architektur*, Munich 1925). In 1924 Arthur Korn became
secretary of the November Group. The following essay was his first
publication.

Architecture is symbol. Nimbus. Tendency to organization – music, towards
an impetus that carries right through to the end. Embrace and dissolution.
The house is no longer a block, only dissolution into cells, crystallization
from point to point, the construction of bridges, joints, outer surfaces, tubes.
Outer surfaces that envelop air, that expel air. Air sinks down between them
as fruit prunes canes. Air has streamed into them and makes them firm and
pliable.

Architecture is passionate loving. Rearing up. Circling round. Like us pressed
down, jumped up. Symbol. Fiery sign.
   For what turns reality into a work of art is the fiery sign. Burning cities.
Burning landscapes.

Architecture as royal leader. All materials have been given into its hand: iron,
steel and glass, wood and porcelain, fabric and paper. It develops a feeling
for the substance, structure, and construction of every material. Furniture
bursts forth from germinating walls, and the reed huts of the natives have long
ago grown up into fantastic grass towers.

Architecture, meaningful as the machine, as the underground railway – the
air cabin, the motor-car body. Inconspicuously collective.

But the impersonal utilitarian building is only habitable if behind the satisfied
need there stands the symbolic art form that feels the organism and asks:
Upon what points of support, what outer surfaces does the building stand?
How do the areas of light rest inside it, how do the planes stand – straight,
tilted? How do the movable and immovable furnishings link up with it? How
does the artificial light source sit? How does the colour stand or move? How
does the building relate to the close and distant environment, to the atmosphere? How do the individual rooms relate collectively? How does the whole
acquire significance in relation to the smallest part and in what way does the

whole become a cell of the larger community? How does the whole develop into a symbol of the human being and of landscape?

The faceless solution is inadequate. The American – rectilinear – rational city is deadly.

In practice, the impersonal utilitarian building is only habitable if it is constructive. Construction, however, is attained only through analysis. The machine designer also asks first: What task is the machine to fulfil – turning, planing, boring? And if I wish to produce a boring action, I need the rotating movement. He first analyses and then constructs.

The architect also begins with an analysis of the building programme, the dwelling, the factory. He discovers parts, rooms, cells. He fashions the communications, the horizontal tubes, the vertical stair towers. He discovers the focal points and fixes them like the centre-bit on the plane disc.

He discovers the primal cell that is peculiar to every organism, every house, and every town and to it alone, and that stamps all its forms. He analyses the material, its inner construction, its strength, its structure.

He analyses the whole construction, upon which everything stands, the thin supports and discs in the nucleus, and hangs around it the outer wall with its apertures. Thus he analyses every factor that plays a part.

And only then does he build up the construction.

Interlocking of the material body and the spherical air space above it. Entry of air into the body-mass and envelopment of the body with wires that produce new air planes. Arms, stretched out from the centre into the air, and ribs, grown through the floor.

Analytical building, utilizing the ultimate secrets of the material, the construction, the cellular organization, and intercommunications, is the indispensable prerequisite. It is the basis – no less, and no more.

But then it is a matter of art to create the total work in a completely original way, as though it had just come into the world.

A mystical happening according to unknown, unconscious laws and yet a concrete event, which mysteriously recreates the first rational procedure in a spiritual realm of its own.

There remains the incomprehensible mystery that the razor-sharp analytical construction and the Utopia born in the realm of the unconscious intersect at one point, as though the unconscious genius in us repeated the creative process again to the same end on a higher plane unknown to us.

The symbol and the fiery sign in us is as concrete as the analytical construction. And not only in me. The conflict between the machine-man and the anarchistic-artistic man, between the collective and the individual personality that organizes itself freely and in accordance with mystic laws, like the voice of music, repeats on a larger scale the rise from the necessary constructive–analytical reality to the intuitive-artistic one.

1924 Theo van Doesburg: Towards a plastic architecture

In Paris, Theo van Doesburg once again – and not for the last time – formulated his theory of elemental construction. After his stays in Weimar, where in 1922 he gave courses in the immediate proximity of the Bauhaus – 'from 1921 to 1923 Neo-Plasticism, from the two centres Weimar and Berlin, dominated the whole of modern design' – he settled in Paris. During November/December 1923 a big De Stijl exhibition was held in the Galerie de l'Effort Moderne, which brought the young Paris architects into contact with the De Stijl movement. A demonstration of the new domestic architecture was organized by van Doesburg in Paris in spring 1924.

1. Form. Elimination of all *concept of form* in the sense of a *fixed type* is essential to the healthy development of architecture and art as a whole. Instead of using earlier styles as models and imitating them, the problem of architecture must be posed entirely afresh.

2. The new architecture is *elemental*; that is to say, it develops out of the elements of building in the widest sense. These elements – such as function, mass, surface, time, space, light, colour, material, etc. – are *plastic*.

3. The new architecture is *economic*; that is to say, it employs its elemental means as effectively and thriftily as possible and squanders neither these means nor the material.

4. The new architecture is *functional*; that is to say, it develops out of the exact determination of the practical demands, which it contains within clear outlines.

5. The new architecture is *formless* and yet exactly defined; that is to say, it is not subject to any fixed aesthetic formal type. It has no mould (such as confectioners use) in which it produces the functional surfaces arising out of practical, living demands.

In contradistinction to all earlier styles the new architectural methods know no closed type, no *basic type*.

The functional space is strictly divided into rectangular surfaces having no individuality of their own. Although each one is fixed on the basis of the others, they may be visualized as extending infinitely. Thus they form a co-ordinated system in which all points correspond to the same number of points in the universe. It follows from this that the surfaces have a direct connexion to infinite space.

6. The new architecture has rendered the concept *monumental* independent of large and small (since the word 'monumental' has become hackneyed it is replaced by the word 'plastic'). It has shown that everything exists on the basis of interrelationships.

7. The new architecture possesses no single *passive factor*. It has overcome the *opening* (in the wall). With its *openness* the window plays an active role in opposition to the *closedness* of the wall surface. Nowhere does an opening or a gap occupy the foreground; everything is strictly determined by contrast. Compare the various counter-constructions in which the elements that architecture consists of (surface, line, and mass) are placed without constraint in a three-dimensional relationship.

8. *The ground-plan*. The new architecture has *opened* the walls and so done away with the separation of *inside* and *outside*. *The walls themselves no longer support*; they merely provide supporting points. The result is a new, open ground-plan entirely different from the classical one, since inside and outside now pass over into one another.

9. The new architecture is *open*. The whole structure consists of a space that is divided in accordance with the various functional demands. This division is carried out by means of *dividing surfaces* (in the interior) or *protective surfaces* (externally). The former, which separate the various functional spaces, may be *movable*; that is to say, the dividing surfaces (formerly the interior walls) may be replaced by movable intermediate surfaces or panels (the same method may be employed for doors). In architecture's next phase of development the ground-plan must disappear completely. The two-dimensional spatial composition *fixed* in a ground-plan will be replaced by an exact *constructional calculation* – a calculation by means of which the supporting capacity is restricted to the simplest but strongest supporting points. For this purpose Euclidean mathematics will be of no further use – but with the aid of calculation that is non-Euclidean and takes into account the four dimensions everything will be very easy.

10. *Space and time*. The new architecture takes account not only of space but also of the magnitude *time*. Through the unity of space and time the architectural exterior will acquire a new and completely plastic aspect. (Four-dimensional space-time aspects.)

11. The new architecture is *anti-cubic*; that is to say, it does not attempt to fit all the functional space cells together into a closed cube, but *projects functional space-cells* (as well as overhanging surfaces, balconies, etc.) centrifugally from the centre of the cube outwards. Thus height, breadth, and depth plus time gain an entirely new plastic expression. In this way architecture achieves a more or less floating aspect (in so far as this is possible from the constructional standpoint – this is a problem for the engineer!) which operates, as it were, in opposition to natural gravity.

12. *Symmetry and repetition*. The new architecture has eliminated both monotonous repetition and the stiff equality of two halves – the mirror image, symmetry. There is no repetition in time, no street front, no standardization.

A block of houses is just as much a whole as the individual house. The laws that apply to the individual house also apply to the block of houses and to the city. In place of symmetry the new architecture offers *a balanced relationship of unequal parts*; that is to say, of parts that differ from each other by virtue of their functional characteristics as regards position, size, proportion and situation. The equality of these parts rests upon the balance of their dissimilarity, not upon their similarity. Furthermore, the new architecture has rendered front, back, right, left, top, and bottom, factors of equal value.

13. In contrast to frontalism, which had its origin in a rigid, static way of life, the new architecture offers the plastic richness of an all-sided development in space and time.

14. *Colour.* The new architecture has done away with painting as a separate and imaginary expression of harmony, secondarily as representation, primarily as coloured surface.

The new architecture permits colour organically as a direct means of expressing its relationships within space and time. Without colour these relationships are not real, but *invisible.* The balance of organic relationships acquires visible reality only by means of colour. The modern painter's task consists in creating with the aid of colour a harmonious whole in the new four-dimensional realm of space-time – not a surface in two dimensions. In a further phase of development colour may also be replaced by a denaturalized material possessing its own specific colour (a problem for the chemist) – but only if practical needs demand this material.

15. The new architecture is *anti-decorative.* Colour (and this is something the colour-shy must try to grasp) is not a decorative part of architecture, but its organic medium of expression.

16. *Architecture as a synthesis of Neo-Plasticism.* Building is a part of the new architecture which, by combining together all the arts in their elemental manifestation, discloses their true nature.

A prerequisite is the ability to think in four dimensions – that is to say: the architects of Plasticism, among whom I also number the painters, must construct within the new realm of space and time.

Since the new architecture permits no images (such as paintings or sculptures as separate elements) its purpose of creating a harmonious whole with all essential means is evident from the *outset.* In this way, every architectural element contributes to the attainment on a practical and logical basis of a maximum of plastic expression, without any disregard of the practical demands.

1924   Ludwig Mies van der Rohe: Industrialized building

In the third edition of G (10 June 1924) Mies van der Rohe, using his own concise style of expression, demanded a fundamental revision of the whole building industry. The demand for economy of materials and constructions, made a year earlier in the first issue of G, was now extended to the whole building process, beginning with the manufacture of new building materials and ending with mere assembly work on the site. For the first time with such unequivocal clarity attention was directed not exclusively to the result – architecture – but also to the prerequisites for industrialized forms of building.

A little while ago the need for an industrialization of the building trade was still contested by almost all interested parties, and I regard it as progress that this question is now seriously discussed by a larger circle, even if few of those concerned are really convinced of this need. The increasing industrialization in all fields would also have spread to the building trade with no regard for outmoded outlooks and emotional values, if special circumstances had not here barred the way. I see in industrialization the central problem of building in our time. If we succeed in carrying out this industrialization, the social, economic, technical, and also artistic problems will be readily solved. The question of how industrialization is to be introduced is easily answered once we know what stands in the way. The supposition that antiquated forms of organization are the cause is incorrect. They are not the cause but the effect of a situation, and they in no way clash with the character of the old building trade. Repeated attempts have been made to arrive at new forms of organization, but they have succeeded only in those parts of the trade that permitted industrialization. Moreover the extent to which modern building has become a matter of assembly has undoubtedly been exaggerated. Prefabrication has been carried out almost exclusively in the construction of hangars for industry and agriculture, and it was the iron foundries that first prefabricated parts for assembly on the site. Recently timber firms have also begun to prefabricate parts so that building shall be a matter purely of assembly. In almost all other buildings the whole of the main frame and large parts of the interior have been constructed in the same manner since time immemorial and are entirely manual in character. This character can be changed neither by economic forms nor by working methods and it is precisely this which renders small undertakings viable. Naturally material and wages can be saved by the use of larger and different types of building units, as new methods of building show; but even this in no way changes the manual character of building. Moreover it must be borne in mind that the brick wall has incontestable advantages over these new methods of construction.

It is not so much a question of rationalizing existing working methods as of fundamentally remoulding the whole building trade.

So long as we use essentially the same materials, the character of building will not change, and this character, as I have already mentioned, ultimately determines the forms taken by the trade. Industrialization of the building trade is a question of material. Hence the demand for a new building material is the first prerequisite. Our technology must and will succeed in inventing a building material that can be manufactured technologically and utilized industrially, that is solid, weather-resistant, soundproof, and possessed of good insulating properties. It will have to be a light material whose utilization does not merely permit but actually invites industrialization. Industrial production of all the parts can really be rationalized only in the course of the manufacturing process, and work on the site will be entirely a matter of assembly and can be restricted to a far shorter time than was ever thought possible. This will result in greatly reduced building costs. Moreover the new trends in architecture will find their true tasks. It is quite clear to me that this will lead to the total destruction of the building trade in the form in which it has existed up to now; but whoever regrets that the house of the future can no longer be constructed by building craftsmen should bear in mind that the motor-car is no longer built by the wheelwright.

1924 Hermann Finsterlin: Casa Nova

'Architecture of the Future – Play of Forms and Subtle Construction' was the subtitle given by Hermann Finsterlin (b.1887 in Munich, lives in Stuttgart) to his essay which took up the whole March 1924 issue of the Amsterdam periodical *Wendingen*. His architectural fantasies had already aroused considerable interest in 1919, when Gropius invited Finsterlin to take part in his Exhibition for Unknown Architects (p.46). Bruno Taut printed two longish contributions by him in *Frühlicht* in 1920–1. The relatively late publication in *Wendingen* – in terms of the general trend – shows that the Architectura et Amicitia group was still asserting its viewpoint (knowledge through vision) against De Stijl in 1924.

Awake! Awake from the compulsive sleep into which you children of Adam have been plunged by the unripe fruit of the world tree and pluck your divine happiness, now never to be lost again, from its infinite branches: the knowledge of the primal meaning of all being – 'development'. Life is the unconscious answer to stimuli, experience is human existence. The value of a life follows from the sum of the creature's experience in Creation; therefore the duration of a life and the course it takes are not matters of indifference. Adjust your sieve to the measure of your highest will, so that all inadequacies and compromises filter through it; they are not worth retaining. Do not give preference to line and surface, which make you conscious of the corporeal; this is ingratitude towards the heritage of the creature. Do not beat the drum where the bellows of a gigantic organ await you; do not imitate – that which has *once* existed has no need of repetitions, they are always feebly degenerate and merely a waste of your time. Cease to invent, it merely robs you of your eyes. Why do you strive to broaden your senses? The mania for discovery is merely poverty of imagination and creative power. There is nothing beyond your outward senses that you could not create with your inmost primal sense, that miniature version of the cosmos, the mightiest wonder of human existence. Discover this philosophers' stone that renders you all-powerful like the world spirit.

The apparent basic difference between things lies only in you and in your temporal and spatial distances from them, only in the measurement of time arising out of your organic mechanism. This alone creates the antitheses of space and time, matter and energy, rest and motion, life and death. Push on to the centre point of the world and you will find yourselves again, in changed shape, at the root of the world tree, in whose sap appearance and being flow into one.

Everything has *form* – is *form:*
Radiations, scents, sounds, and the most mysterious sensations of the soul. Form is only a relatively over-rapid, uninterrupted system of forces flowing

within a closed movement and developing in a relatively close-meshed manner within four-dimensional space, its peculiar material manifestation the consequence of its own speed and multiplicity and the playful struggle it is waging with the objects of space, with the pressure of light, and all the surgings of the most subtle spirits; a pressure imparted by mutually motivating densities that flow forward and back, modify or interpenetrate each other, arrange themselves according to selective affinities. This path of struggle will always be marked by halting places, nodal points, since the energy waves, no matter how confusingly manifold they may be, come into equilibrium. These are the architectonic moments in world events. In the realm of the infinitely small and the infinitely large there are in every particle of time an infinite number of such 'buildings'. But none of the earthly planes could measure itself against the structures refined in the fire of the essential human tools. We earthlings can discern the manifestations of refined forces only in a few small objects of nature firmly determined by formulae – in twinned crystals or glacial erosions, in over-cultivated flowers and the skeletal joints of the higher animals; but we entirely lack the inner impression of the small-scale environment, since the landscape, above all mountains, is scarcely apprehended as a unitary spatial experience and the causal forces of rock and ice caves do not provide formal refinements of the highest kind. Just tell me then why man has never yet created for himself the wonderful space incomparably rich in stimuli, the solidified echoes of a rich and unique soul?

I beg you to lay aside the illusion that the purpose of human building is to create dwelling-places, that is to say sheltering caverns, for objects, plants, animals, men, and gods. All predetermined purpose falls like a heavy, inhibiting hand upon the motive force of a divinely free, pure will. Forget that you exist, create vast divine vessels, and when a solemn hour of your souls takes on a rigid skin, then dedicate this monument as the permanent womb of your body or of that of your fellow men. Human space – no longer the hollow impression of a few elementary stereometric bodies, but a glacier-grinding system of the soul, not the product of nature spirits determined by earthly metabolism but stubbornly ground out by the finest millstones of the human soul or hollowed out in an instant by the greatest possible heat and pressure like a geode in the rock. Light sources the thinnest places between proliferating matter, the motionless vessel-substitutes constituted by the old furniture made up of foreign bodies – the floor, only more a co-operation on the part of the plane held forcibly horizontal that relates the most enchanting stories of form to the newly discovered sensitivities of the soles of our feet. The first truly specific shelter of the highest animal species, to which it has been entitled ever since it became human – the maternally satisfying 'organ' of a huge and ghostly organism, now rendered independent and visible, though for the time being still crudely material, the child of man's first natural 'dwelling'. (The shell of a divine animal with a fabulous corporeal relief, which vanished like a being composed of soft material tired of materiality, came to life again and inherited only the faultlessly stabilized depth-image of its testimony to life.) Seal of the soul that gives everyone blind to the world around him the echo of his inner voice, bringing him a happiness which the crudity of the lowest spatial class is simply not able to produce.

Did the builders, banished to the roots, forget that the tree of development is continued across the earth in limitless ramification, division, refinement down to the formula governing the growth of blossoms? Could such a nameless incest otherwise have so degraded human architecture that, like a defective barrel organ, it repeats the first bars of a popular song of form, the first bars of a symphony of form that is as infinite as the universe? The ABC of physical form and the modest links between this trinity remained the stammering vocabulary of human architecture until our own day. The three allotropic states of the primal shape, the sphere – its movement towards a goal in the cone and the path into the infinite in the astragal, approaching the resistance effects of the polyhedron in the polyvertex and the polygon. These few characteristics of the primal shape have coupled to form the first hybrids, uniting, interpenetrating or splitting up; but these half-breeds remained infertile through the millenia, the decision to create the boundless *varieties of 'form in itself'* through progressive combination of the most manifold bodies, increasingly rich in the parts of which they are composed, was not taken. Up to the present, building has consisted in the breaking down of forms.

Show me how you built and I shall tell you who you were. Do you nations hear the judgement of the judge Clio? (Individuals can deceive, countless motives determine the nature of the dwelling in which they clothe themselves, but a single nation during a single cultural period cannot fail to express itself; its architectural organs will reveal the degree of its feeling as expressed in the material and allot it its place on the evolutionary ladder, its branch on the family tree of the living.) We have been moulded by the machine for centuries, but beyond this positive dance of death, this unregarded single-plane, single-track skeletal development, this misunderstood incorporealization, whose inertia factor, the equilibrium of architecture, was set free from the nauseating popular-song repetition of *one* formula of motion, the god of the earth will recall his noble mission. (The best thing about the machine was at most the construction of its members, the first attempt at formal refinement.) Was it a god who wrote this sign? This enthusiastic question asked by posterity ought to have been the lifelong ambition of every builder when his pencil was guided by the pulses of the most central spirit, when he planted the hieroglyphic seed for an eighth wonder of the world.

Building is the experience of space; inspiration, invention, the clearest, most sudden awareness of the soul's echo in the primeval jungle of the environment; a purposeless, unexampled play of the finest forces in porous matter whose flux came to a standstill in a moment of highest reflection, oblivious of pleasure, existing in appearance only, a waking sleep of forces, a *stationary movement* that might at any time continue to flower in all directions or disintegrate into well-shaped component parts, spontaneously splitting up like a living crystal without beginning or end like everything through which there quivers the pulse of the eternal. I tell you such a structure will please the eye like Memnon's granite body when the sun caresses it with its wakeful gaze, such a vessel must be fragrant as the blossom that surrenders itself to the light flooding from the full moon – such a thing must play colourless in colours like the intricate pattern of a thousand rainbows – because it is the immediate primal and eternal, universal expression of being. (The final victory of the nobility of being over the mass rule of repetition which at best simulated a modest variation in front of distorting mirrors or sought unviable hybrids in out-of-keeping revivals and compulsive deformations.)

And the day will come when grand *simplicity* will once again dawn with its everlasting calm, this highest possible intensification of reality which we are just still able to imagine. This simplicity has little to do with the naïveté of our present-day constructions. Above and beyond the so-called 'formless' state which does not exist, because just this state is the most evolved and formally most mature as a result of the countless effects that granulate its raised and lowered relief most finely to the point of apparent unity; above and beyond the imagined chaos that bears within and without itself an infinite number of standpoints whose approximations reveal to themselves the closely concealed superpositions in the most pleasurable and agonizingly ecstatic riches (for statics is only a fermata in the flow of shape-notes of the dynamic), extreme splitting up repeats in the realm of the spiritually huge the figure of its first smallest primal image; unconscious restriction of absolutely human characteristics, of the most refined supra-personal formulae. Then too the day has come when those who know slumber wakefully under the dome of melting stars or under the protective vault of natural caves, in the godlike feeling of the uninterruptible omnipotence of their imagination (or consciously embracing the unexcellable apparition of their image of likeness in the most knowledgeable love).

But first we must travel the long, agonizingly blissful path, the *détour* back to paradise. *Etiam architectura non facit saltus!* But first the giant baby architecture must develop so that it learns to walk *this* path.

(Do you ask about the technical means of this architecture that does not seem to be of this world? Where there is a will there is a way. Think of the enormous cave sculptures of the Incas, of the monolithic temples of India, of the possibilities of iron and artificial stone, and the gigantic glass flux of the future. The means that are called upon to give shape to such a wealth of physical appearance will have to be correspondingly multifarious.)

1924 Kasimir Malevich: Suprematist manifesto Unovis (excerpt)

On 2 May 1924 Kasimir Malevich (b.1878 near Kiev, d.1935 in Leningrad) published his *Suprematist Manifesto*, to which he attached the abbreviation Unovis: 'Establishment of new forms of art'. Already in winter 1915–16 Malevich's *Black Square on White Ground* hung in the 'last Futurist exhibition "0.10" ' in St Petersburg as a guiding image for new forms, the 'Zero Form' or 'naked unframed icon of my time' (Malevich). His book *Die gegenstandslose Welt* (first published by the Bauhaus in 1927 and published in an English translation in 1959 as *The Non-Objective World*) grew in the confusion of the years of war and revolution in Russia. Gabo and Pevsner, Kandinsky, Lissitzky, and Moholy-Nagy carried Suprematism into Europe with them as a catalyst.

The art of the present, and in particular painting, has been victorious on the whole front. Consciousness has overcome the flat surface and advanced to the art of creation in space. Henceforth the painting of pictures will be left to those who have been unable, despite tireless labour, to free their consciousness from the flat surface, those whose consciousness has remained flat because it could not overcome the flat surface.

Through spatial consciousness painting has developed into the constructive creation of form.

In order to find a system for the spatial orders, it is necessary to do away with all dying systems of the past, with all their accretions, by advancing unflaggingly along the new path . . .

Our path will be difficult, very difficult! The *vis inertiae* of economic and aesthetic concepts is positively unshakable. Therefore Futurism too, with its dynamism, fought against all clinging to yesterday. This struggle was the sole guarantee of the timely dissolution of these things. But aesthetics too, that mendacious emotional concept, declared implacable war on the new art. Since 1913 this struggle has been carried on more intensely under the motto of Suprematism as the 'non-objective world-view'!

Life must be purified of the clutter of the past, of parasitical eclecticism, so that it can be brought to its normal evolution.

Victory of today over fond habits presupposes dismissal of yesterday, the clearing of consciousness from rubbish . . . Everything that still belongs to yesterday is eclectic: the cart, the primitive plough, the horse, cottage industries, landscape painting, statues of liberty, triumphal arches, factory meals, and – above all – buildings in the classical style.

Everything is eclecticism looked at from the age of the aeroplane and radio. Even the motor-car really belongs in the lumber room already, in the graveyard of eclecticism, like the telegraph and the telephone. The new dwellings of man lie in space. The Earth is becoming for him an intermediate stage; accordingly airfields must be built suited to the aeroplane, that is to say without columnar architecture.

The new man's provisional dwellings both in space and on Earth must be adapted to the aeroplane. A house built in this way will still be habitable tomorrow. Hence we Suprematists propose the objectless planets as a basis for the common creation of our existence. We Suprematists will seek allies for the struggle against outmoded forms of architecture . . .

If the Leningrad of the future were built in the style of the American skyscraper cities, then the life style and the thinking of its inhabitants would also correspond to the Americans'. Yet among ourselves ever greater efforts are being made to squeeze present-day existence into an antique mould . . .

The forms of classical antiquity, they say, are important, and only idiots could fail to recognize their value for the proletariat. But where then is the aeroplane, or even merely the motor-car, to be housed? How can modern technology be expressed in antique forms?

We Suprematists therefore accept the fate of being considered idiots and dispute the necessity of antique forms for our time. We emphatically refuse to be pressed into antique moulds.

We don't want to be firemen whose legs are clad in modern trousers, but whose heads are embellished by the helmets of Roman legionaries; we don't want to be like those Negroes upon whom English culture bestowed the umbrella and the top hat, and we don't want our wives to run around naked like savages in the garb of Venus!

We recognize the grandeur of classical art. We don't deny that it was great for its time.

Nor do we dispute that the proletariat must get to know classical antiquity and acquire the right attitude to it. But we dispute very emphatically that classical antiquity is still fitted to our modern world.

Every new idea demands the new form appropriate to it.

Therefore we refuse to recognize classical temples, which were adequate both for the pagans and for the Christians, as now suitable for club houses or a 'House of Culture' for the proletariat, even if these temples are called after the leaders of the Revolution and decorated with their pictures!

We want to create new relationships to the content of today, relationships that do not move on the plane of classical antiquity, but on the plane of the present, of today!

We regard the form of aestheticizing representational painting as finished. Suprematism has shifted the emphasis of its activity to the architectural front and calls upon all revolutionary architects to join it.

1925   Le Corbusier:
Guiding principles of town planning

Le Corbusier's fundamental essay on town planning (*Urbanisme*) appeared in the *Collection de l'Esprit Nouveau* in 1925. Once again – as in *Vers une Architecture* – there is a programmatic statement; once again the individual chapters are prefaced by guiding principles. The sensational *Plan Voisin* for Paris, for 'a city of the present with three million inhabitants', had been in existence since 1922. It had never ceased to preoccupy town planners since its appearance. Now Le Corbusier drew conceptual consequences, linking axioms with events of the day in his own enthusiastic manner. 'I felt very clearly that events were pressing. 1922–5 – how fast everything moved!'

If it yearns after primordial truths,
the spirit destroys itself;
if it weds the earth it thrives.
Max Jacob (*Philosophies*, No.1, 1924)

The town is a working tool.

Towns do not normally fulfil this function. They are inefficient: they wear out the body, they frustrate the mind.

The increasing disorder in our towns is offensive: their decay damages our self-esteem and injures our dignity.

They are not worthy of the age. They are no longer worthy of us.

A town!

It is an assault by man upon nature. It is a human action against nature, a human organism designed for shelter and work. It is a creation.

Poetry is a human act – concerted interrelationships between perceptible images. To be exact, the poetry of nature is nothing but a construction of the human spirit. The town is a powerful image that activates our spirit. Why should not the town, even today, be a source of poetry?

Geometry is the means with which we have provided ourselves for looking around us and expressing ourselves.

Geometry is the basis.

It is also the material foundation for symbols signifying perfection, the divine.

It brings us the lofty satisfaction of mathematics.

The machine develops out of geometry. Thus the whole of the modern age is made up above all of geometry; it directs its dreams towards the joys of geometry. After a century of analysis, modern arts and thought are seeking something beyond the random fact and geometry leads them towards a mathematical order, an attitude of mind that is increasingly widespread.

The house poses the problem of architecture afresh by calling for totally new means of realization, an entirely new ground-plan adapted to a new way of life, an aesthetic arising out of a new frame of mind. There comes a time when a collective passion stirs an epoch (the Pan-Germanism of 1900–20, or the charity of the first Christians, etc.)

This passion animates actions, gives them a strong tinge and a direction.

Today this passion is the passion for precision. Precision carried a very long way and elevated to the status of an ideal: the striving for perfection.

It is no good being defeatist if one is striving after precision. This requires stubborn courage and strength of character. Our era is no longer one of relaxation and slackness. It is powerfully tensed for action. Whatever one does, it is no good being defeatist (or foolish or disenchanted). We must believe; we must reach down to the good in the depths of people.

It is no good being defeatist if we are going to dream of modern town planning, because this involves overturning many accepted ideas. But today we may dream of carrying out modern town planning, because the time has come and a collective passion has been unleashed by the most brutal necessity and by a lofty feeling for truth. The awakened spirit is already reconstructing the social framework.

It seems that a series of experiments are pointing to the solution and that hypothetical concepts are strongly rooted in statistical truths. A time is coming when a collective passion will be capable of stirring an epoch.

Last year I was working on this book in the vacuum of a Paris summer. This temporary slackening of the life of the great city, this calm, finally began to make me feel that I was allowing myself to be carried away by the magnitude of the subject, carried beyond the reality.

Came 1 October. At dusk, at six o'clock on the Champs-Elysées, everything suddenly went mad. After the vacuum, the traffic furiously started up again. Then each day increased this turmoil further. You go out and the moment you are out of the door, with no transition, you are confronting death: the cars are racing past. Twenty years ago I was a student. In those days the roadway belonged to us; we sang in it, we argued . . . the horse bus rolled gently past.

That 1 October 1924, on the Champs-Elysées, we watched the event, the titanic rebirth of this new thing whose vigour had been broken by three months of holidays: the traffic. Cars, cars, speed, speed! One is carried away, seized by enthusiasm, by joy. Not by enthusiasm at seeing the shiny bodywork glistening in the light of the headlamps. But enthusiasm over the joy of power. The frank, ingenuous enjoyment of being at the centre of power, of energy. We share in this power. We are part of this society whose dawn is breaking. We have confidence in this new society, confidence that it will find the magnificent expression of its energy. We believe in it.

Its energy is like a torrent swollen by storms: a destructive fury. The town is breaking in pieces, the town cannot last, the town is no good any longer. The town is too old. The torrent has no bed. Then there is a kind of cataclysm.

It is something absolutely abnormal: the balance is upset more and more each day.

Now the danger is felt by everyone. Let us note in passing that in a few years the joy of living has already been forgotten (the good, centuries-old joy of strolling tranquilly along on one's legs); we are caught up in the attitude of a hunted animal, in a daily fight for life;[1] the sign has changed; the normality of existence has been destroyed, has become marked by the negative sign.

Timid remedies are put forward... You know the childish ardour with which the inhabitants of a village erect improvised barriers, in haste and terror, to hold back the torrent that has swollen under the effects of the storm and is already rolling along destruction in its furiously swirling waters...

Fifteen years ago, in the course of long journeys, I measured the omnipotent force of architecture, but I had to pass through difficult stages in order to find the necessary environment. Architecture submerged beneath a deluge of disconnected heritages attracted the spirit only via a difficult detour and stirred the emotions only weakly. By contrast, an architecture firmly rooted in its environment gave rise to a delightful sense of harmony and stirred one deeply. Confronted by the facts and far from all text-books, I felt the presence of an essential factor, *town planning*, an expression unknown to me at the time.

I was entirely devoted to art.

There was a time when the reading of Camillo Sitte,[2] the Viennese, insidiously won me over to the picturesque view of the city. Sitte's arguments were skilful, his theories seemed correct; they were based on the past. In fact, they were the past – and the miniature past, the sentimental past, the rather insignificant little flower by the roadside. This was not the past of apogees; it was the past of compromises. Sitte's eloquence went well with this touching renaissance of the 'home' which, in a paradox worthy of the cottage, was destined grotesquely to divert architecture from its proper path ('regionalism').

In 1922, when I was commissioned by the Salon d'Automne to design the diorama of a city of three million inhabitants, I entrusted myself to the sure paths of reason and having digested the lyricism of days gone by, I had the feeling that I was in harmony with that of our own day, which I love.

My close friends, surprised to see me deliberately overstep immediate possibilities, said to me: 'Are you designing for the year 2000?' Everywhere journalists wrote of 'the city of the future'. And yet I had named this work 'A Contemporary City' – contemporary, because tomorrow belongs to no one.

I felt very clearly that events were pressing. 1922–5, how fast everything moved!

1925: the International Exhibition of Decorative Arts in Paris finally demonstrated the pointlessness of backward glances. There was to be a complete revulsion; a new page was turned.

---

[1] This is precisely true; we risk our lives at every step. Suppose your foot slips, or a fainting fit causes you to stumble...
[2] *Der Städtebau.*

It is generally agreed that 'sublime' futilities are followed by serious works.

Decorative art is dead. Modern town planning is born with a new architecture. An immense, devastating, brutal evolution has burned the bridges that link us with the past.

Recently, a young Viennese architect – terribly disillusioned – admitted that old Europe was on the verge of dying, that young America alone could nourish our hopes.

'No architectural problem any longer confronts us in Europe', he said. 'Up to this day we have dragged ourselves along on our knees, weighed down, crushed by the tangled burden of successive cultures. The Renaissance, then the two Louis have exhausted us. We are too rich; we are surfeited; we no longer possess the virginity that can give rise to an architecture.'

'The problem of architecture in old Europe', I replied to him, 'is the big modern city. It is a matter of *Yes* or *No*, of life or slow extinction. One or the other, but it will be the former if we *wish*. And precisely the past cultures that weigh us down will afford us the pure, distilled solution, passed through all the sieves of reason and the sensibility of an élite.'

Faced with the 1922 diorama the director of the New York *Broom* said to me: 'In two hundred years Americans will come and admire the rational works of modern France and the French will go to be amazed by the romantic skyscrapers of New York.'

Summary:

Between believing and not believing, it is better to believe.

Between acting and disintegrating, it is better to act.

To be young and full of health means to be able to produce a great deal, but it takes years of experience to be able to produce well.

To be nourished by earlier civilizations enables us to dissipate obscurity and bring a clear judgement to bear on things. It is defeatist to say that once one has left one's student days behind one is nothing but a has-been. They decide that we are old? Old? The twentieth century in Europe may be the fine maturity of a civilization. Old Europe is not old at all. Those are just words. Old Europe is full of vigour. Our spirit, nourished by centuries, is alert and inventive. Europe's strength is in her head, whereas America has strong arms and the noble sentimentality of adolescence. If in America they produce and feel, in Europe we think.

There is no reason to bury old Europe.

Man strides straight ahead because he has a goal. He knows where he is going; he has decided in favour of a particular direction and is striding straight towards it.

The set square is the necessary and sufficient tool for action, because it serves to determine space with absolute unambiguity.

A flood of action which leaves purposes way behind it, taking shape according to the special capacities of the peoples, stirs the emotions and comes to dominate developments; it issues orders; it firmly establishes behaviour and gives events their deeper significance.

At first this flood of action disappoints; but on closer consideration it encourages and arouses confidence. The great works of industry do not call for great men.

Let us take care that the enemy of joy – despair – does not slip in unnoticed. Despair over cities. Despair engendered by cities.

A Turkish proverb: Where you build, there you plant trees.

In our case we cut them down.

And what about motor cars?

So much the better, replied the great aedile, they won't be able to drive any more.

Statistics show the past and sketch the future; they furnish figures and give the direction of curves.

Statistics serve the purpose of setting problems.

The machine gives our dreams their audacity: they can be realized.

We need a guideline. We need basic principles for modern town planning. We need to advance through the construction of a theoretical edifice of the utmost stringency to the formulation of the basic principles for modern town planning.

The city of speed is the city of success.

On 9 May 1925 half the chestnut trees along the Avenue des Champs-Elysées had black leaves; the buds could not unfold; the tiny, crippled leaves curled up like the bent fingers of a hand . . .

It is assumed that the third generation to live in a big city will be sterile.

At the present moment, vast masses of dilapidated houses are being demolished at strategically important points in Paris and replaced by multi-storey buildings.

This is being allowed to happen. A new city is being permitted to spring up over the old city that murdered life, and this new city will murder life all the more infallibly because it forms positive knots of stasis, without in any way modifying the street-plan.

These fruitless operations on the land in the centre of Paris are like a cancer that is being allowed to overgrow the heart of the city. The cancer will stifle the city. Simply to let things happen here represents an incomprehensible unconcern in the hour of danger, through which big cities are at present passing.

'They are drawing straight lines, filling in holes, levelling off and coming to Nihilism . . .' (sic!) (Furious outburst by the great town planner presiding over a commission for city extension plans.)

I replied: 'I beg your pardon, but that, correctly speaking, is man's task.' (Authentic incident.) Extract from the documents *Cacophony*.

1926 Walter Gropius:
Principles of Bauhaus production [Dessau]
(excerpt)

In September 1922 Feininger asked in Weimar: 'Why and how this voluntary submission to the tyranny of van Doesburg and the complete recalcitrance towards all measures originating from the Bauhaus?' He meant by this the effects of the 'rival courses' given by van Doesburg in Weimar. 'If Doesburg were a teacher at the Bauhaus he would be . . . rather useful to the whole enterprise.' The fascination of De Stijl ideas not only captured the students, but also influenced the Bauhaus teachers. As early as 1923 (in a letter of 5 October) Feininger noted how Gropius's attitude to handicrafts and industrial products was changing. In 1925, with the transfer to Dessau, this process was complete.

The Bauhaus wants to serve in the development of present-day housing, from the simplest household appliances to the finished dwelling.

In the conviction that household appliances and furnishings must be rationally related to each other, the Bauhaus is seeking – by systematic practical and theoretical research in the formal, technical and economic fields – to derive the design of an object from its natural functions and relationships.

Modern man, who no longer dresses in historical garments but wears modern clothes, also needs a modern home appropriate to him and his time, equipped with all the modern devices of daily use.

An object is defined by its nature. In order, then, to design it to function correctly – a container, a chair, or a house – one must first of all study its nature; for it must serve its purpose perfectly, that is, it must fulfil its function usefully, be durable, economical and 'beautiful'. This research into the nature of objects leads to the conclusion that by resolute consideration of modern production methods, constructions, and materials, forms will evolve that are often unusual and surprising, since they deviate from the conventional (consider, for example, the changes in the design of heating and lighting fixtures).

It is only through constant contact with newly evolving techniques, with the discovery of new materials and with new ways of putting things together, that the creative individual can learn to bring the design of objects into a living relationship with tradition and from that point to develop a new attitude toward design, which is:

a resolute affirmation of the living environment of machines and vehicles; the organic design of things based on their own present-day laws, without romantic gloss and wasteful frivolity; the limitation to characteristic, primary forms and colours, readily accessible to everyone; simplicity in multiplicity, economical utilization of space, material, time, and money.

The creation of standard types for all practical commodities of everyday use is a social necessity.

On the whole, the necessities of life are the same for the majority of people. The home and its furnishings are mass consumer goods, and their design is more a matter of reason than a matter of passion. The machine – capable of producing standardized products – is an effective device, which, by means of mechanical aids – steam and electricity – can free the individual from working manually for the satisfaction of his daily needs and can provide him with mass-produced products that are cheaper and better than those manufactured by hand. There is no danger that standardization will force a choice upon the individual, since, due to natural competition, the number of available types of each object will always be ample to provide the individual with a choice of design that suits him best.

The Bauhaus workshops are essentially laboratories in which prototypes of products suitable for mass production and typical of our time are carefully developed and constantly improved.

In these laboratories the Bauhaus wants to train a new kind of collaborator for industry and the crafts, who has an equal command of both technology and form.

To reach the objective of creating a set of standard prototypes which meet all the demands of economy, technology and form, requires the selection of the best, most versatile, and most thoroughly educated men who are well grounded in workshop experience and who are imbued with an exact knowledge of the design elements of form and mechanics and their underlying laws.

The Bauhaus represents the opinion that the contrast between industry and the crafts is much less marked by the difference in the tools they use than by the division of labour in industry and the unity of the work in the crafts. But the two are constantly getting closer to each other. The crafts of the past have changed, and future crafts will be merged in a new productive unity in which they will carry out the experimental work for industrial production. Speculative experiments in laboratory workshops will yield models and prototypes for productive implementation in factories.

The prototypes that have been completed in the Bauhaus workshops are being reproduced by outside firms with whom the workshops are closely related.

The production of the Bauhaus thus does not represent any kind of competition for either industry or crafts but rather provides them with impetus for their development. The Bauhaus does this by bringing creatively talented people with ample practical experience into the actual course of production, to take over the preparatory work for production, from industry and the crafts.

The products reproduced from prototypes that have been developed by the Bauhaus can be offered at a reasonable price only by utilization of all the modern, economical methods of standardization (mass production by industry) and by large-scale sales. The dangers of a decline in the quality of the product by comparison to the prototype, in regard to quality of material and workmanship, as a result of mechanical reproduction will be countered by all available means. The Bauhaus fights against the cheap substitute, inferior workmanship and the dilettantism of the handicrafts, for a new standard of quality work.

1926 Frederick Kiesler: Space City architecture

Theo van Doesburg, in a backward look at the path travelled by De Stijl, related the great interest shown by young architects in the first exhibition of the De Stijl group in Paris at the end of 1923. 'We wanted to bring architecture and painting into the closest possible creative relationship. The house was taken apart, broken down into its plastic elements. The static axis of the old construction was destroyed . . . The house came away free from the ground and the ceiling, as a roof terrace, became as it were an "uncovered" storey.' Frederick Kiesler, one of these young architects (b. 1896 in Vienna, pupil and friend of Adolf Loos, d. 1965 in New York), carried this first step further: no walls, no foundations.

I demand the vital building, the space city, functional architecture:

the building that is adequate to the elasticity of the life function.

1. Transformation of spherical space into cities.

2. To set us free from the ground, the task of the static axis.

3. No walls, no foundations.

4. A building system of tensions in free space.

5. Creation of new possibilities of living and, through them, needs

that will restructure society.

1926 Le Corbusier/Pierre Jeanneret: Five points towards a new architecture

The declaration *Five points towards a new architecture* is roughly contemporaneous with the designs for Le Corbusier's houses in the Weissenhof settlement, Stuttgart, 1927, the second big exhibition of the Deutscher Werkbund. Under the guidance of Mies van der Rohe, who – with the support of comrades-in-arms of the G group, such as Werner Graeff – gave each architect the greatest possible freedom to carry out his ideas, the exhibition became one of the most important events in domestic architecture between the two wars and led directly to the famous Berlin housing estates under Martin Wagner at the end of the twenties.

The theoretical considerations set out below are based on many years of practical experience on building sites.

Theory demands concise formulation.

The following points in no way relate to aesthetic fantasies or a striving for fashionable effects, but concern architectural facts that imply an entirely new kind of building, from the dwelling house to palatial edifices.

1. The supports. To solve a problem scientifically means in the first place to distinguish between its elements. Hence in the case of a building a distinction can immediately be made between the supporting and the non-supporting elements. The earlier foundations, on which the building rested without a mathematical check, are replaced by individual foundations and the walls by individual supports. Both supports and support foundations are precisely calculated according to the burdens they are called upon to carry. These supports are spaced out at specific, equal intervals, with no thought for the interior arrangement of the building. They rise directly from the floor to 3, 4, 6, etc. metres and elevate the ground floor. The rooms are thereby removed from the dampness of the soil; they have light and air; the building plot is left to the garden, which consequently passes under the house. The same area is also gained on the flat roof.

2. The roof gardens. The flat roof demands in the first place systematic utilization for domestic purposes: roof terrace, roof garden. On the other hand, the reinforced concrete demands protection against changing temperatures. Overactivity on the part of the reinforced concrete is prevented by the maintenance of a constant humidity on the roof concrete. The roof terrace satisfies both demands (a rain-dampened layer of sand covered with concrete slabs with lawns in the interstices; the earth of the flowerbeds in direct contact with the layer of sand). In this way the rain water will flow off extremely slowly. Waste pipes in the interior of the building. Thus a latent humidity will remain continually on the roof skin. The roof gardens will display highly luxuriant vegetation. Shrubs and even small trees up to 3 or 4 metres tall can be planted.

In this way the roof garden will become the most favoured place in the building. In general, roof gardens mean to a city the recovery of all the built-up area.

3. The free designing of the ground-plan. The support system carries the intermediate ceilings and rises up to the roof. The interior walls may be placed wherever required, each floor being entirely independent of the rest. There are no longer any supporting walls but only membranes of any thickness required. The result of this is absolute freedom in designing the ground-plan; that is to say, free utilization of the available means, which makes it easy to offset the rather high cost of reinforced concrete construction.

4. The horizontal window. Together with the intermediate ceilings the supports form rectangular openings in the façade through which light and air enter copiously. The window extends from support to support and thus becomes a horizontal window. Stilted vertical windows consequently disappear, as do unpleasant mullions. In this way, rooms are equably lit from wall to wall. Experiments have shown that a room thus lit has an eight times stronger illumination than the same room lit by vertical windows with the same window area.

The whole history of architecture revolves exclusively around the wall apertures. Through use of the horizontal window reinforced concrete suddenly provides the possibility of maximum illumination.

5. Free design of the façade. By projecting the floor beyond the supporting pillars, like a balcony all round the building, the whole façade is extended beyond the supporting construction. It thereby loses its supportive quality and the windows may be extended to any length at will, without any direct relationship to the interior division. A window may just as well be 10 metres long for a dwelling house as 200 metres for a palatial building (our design for the League of Nations building in Geneva). The façade may thus be designed freely.

The five essential points set out above represent a fundamentally new aesthetic. Nothing is left to us of the architecture of past epochs, just as we can no longer derive any benefit from the literary and historical teaching given in schools.

Constructional considerations

Building construction is the purposeful and consistent combination of building elements.

Industries and technological undertakings are being established to deal with the production of these elements.

Serial manufacture enables these elements to be made precise, cheap and good. They can be produced in advance in any number required.

Industries will see to the completion and uninterrupted perfecting of the elements.

Thus the architect has at his disposal a box of building units. His architectural talent can operate freely. It alone, through the building programme, determines his architecture.

The age of the architects is coming.

1927 Ludwig Mies van der Rohe: On form in architecture

This famous letter to Dr Riezler, editor of the Werkbund journal *Die Form*, was published in the journal's second year. If the Stuttgart Weissenhof settlement is a built manifestation of a new style, the inescapable sign of a new will in architecture, then Mies van der Rohe's letter on form in architecture may be looked upon as a still open question: Will life fill the new houses? Will this new architecture be taken up and carried by life, so that a new feeling for life is born of the community-living that takes place in them? The letter throws a bridge across to the theses of Hermann Muthesius and Henry van de Velde and might be said to reconcile the opponents of 1914.

I do not oppose form, but only form as a goal.
And I do this as the result of a number of experiences and the insight I have gained from them.

Form as a goal always ends in formalism.
For this striving is directed not towards an inside, but towards an outside.
But only a living inside has a living outside.

Only intensity of life has intensity of form.
Every How is carried by a What.
The unformed is not worse than the over-formed.
The former is nothing; the latter is mere appearance.
Real form presupposes real life.
But not something that has already existed, nor something thought out.

Here lies the criterion.

We do not evaluate the result but the starting point of the creative process.
Precisely this shows whether the form was discovered by starting from life, or for its own sake.

That is why I consider the creative process so essential.
Life is for us the decisive factor.
In all its fullness, in its spiritual and real commitments.

Is not one of the Werkbund's most important tasks to illuminate, to make visible, the spiritual and real situation in which we stand, to order its currents and thereby to lead the way?
Must we not leave everything else to the creative powers?

1927   Hugo Häring:
Formulations towards a reorientation in the applied arts (excerpt)

'No path necessarily leads from the applied arts to architecture.' Thus Hans Poelzig in 1906. Hugo Häring continued twenty years later in his lecture to the Verein für deutsches Kunstgewerbe (Society for German Arts and Crafts) in Berlin at the beginning of December 1927: 'Work on the house of today is to be regarded as only a preliminary exercise until town planning has undergone the radical transformation called for by the transformation of society and the resulting problems have been finally solved.' For those who did not yet know Häring – then secretary of the Berlin architects' association Der Ring – a new dimension of thinking on all matters of planning and building was opened up.

There are objects which are on the one hand works of art, on the other are intended for use. The fact that they are intended for use cannot always be recognized immediately by a simple person. We call such objects applied art. Many of our museums are filled with products of applied art.

The habit, for thousands of years particularly characteristic of the upper levels of society, of so altering utilitarian objects in the name of art that they became totally unsuited for use is no longer entirely fashionable. We now consider it uncultivated to apply Pallas Athena to the bottom of a bowl; we regard it as tasteless to fashion vessels in the shape of heads or animals and use their interior as containers; we no longer make table legs look like lions' feet.

Today we demand utilitarian objects without adornments, not disguised as something else, free from masking, incrustations. They may nevertheless be noble and exquisite objects, highly valuable products; exquisite quality can be attained without senseless twisting and bending, impressed patterns and the like, which only infringe against the object's essential rights.

The shape of the object is determined by the forms arising out of its purpose, with their own expressive values, and the forms that are created for the sake of a particular expression. Of the form dictated by purpose we may say that it is already given by the elemental laws of the material. A table, a bowl, a knife, a hammer is elemental in its basic form. This basic form is the same all over the world and at all periods.

The form dictated by purpose is the constant element in the object; the problem of expression gives it its ever changing character.

In nature there is no independent problem of appearance; hence there is nothing in opposition to the forms dictated by fitness for purpose. This occurs only among mankind. The essential problem of applied art is clearly that of appearance.

There is no worse enemy of the form dictated by purpose than applied art. The causes may vary, the effect is always the same, namely, violation of the utilitarian object. If we realize this today, a great change must have taken place in us, since in the thousands of years old history of objects this viewpoint has very rarely exercised any effective influence. I see in this fact a moral gain by the present, I regard it as the *sign of a new, evolving culture*. It can also be looked at differently. It may be said that we have become rationalistic, we no longer attach any value to having an Apollo striding across the Greek landscape with his lyre depicted on our teapots . . .

The applied arts or industrial design must be looked at not only from the standpoint of the artist or the craft, but also from that of society. The products of the applied arts are typical creations of society. Without putting it into words, the arts and crafts movement that started thirty years ago was thinking and working for a bourgeois German *middle class*, for essentially *German* conceptions of culture that had arisen in quite specific social strata. The hopes of conquering the world with a new form of applied art were bound to be dashed, since this applied art had absolutely no relationship to these demands of an international society. The world market continued to be dominated by French taste.

Particularly after the war, the expression arts and crafts (*Kunstgewerbe*) had come to have a contemptuous flavour. To say that something was 'arty crafty' implied that it had got stuck at an earlier phase of evolution, that it sprang from the taste of a narrow cultural group and was out of step with an international outlook.

Thirty years ago we could not possibly imagine what the furnishings of a dwelling would look like in 1927 – we are just as unable to imagine today what a house will look like in 1950. Work on the house of today is to be regarded as only a preliminary exercise until town planning has undergone the radical transformation called for by the transformation of society and the resulting problems have been solved. Our present-day building of housing estates is in no way a solution, but a very inadequate expedient. A possible solution must be preceded by a transformation of town planning and this in turn by a transformation in the land question.

Our living rooms have become empty. They now contain only the essentials. Cupboards have been swallowed up in the walls; beds, at least during the day, are beginning to disappear. The architects of the Stuttgart Werkbund Housing Project had the greatest difficulty in finding tables and chairs for their rooms, to say nothing of cupboards, although in Stuttgart and elsewhere thousands and thousands of tables and chairs were standing about in furniture stores and these tables and chairs would undoubtedly have satisfied the *objective* demands made upon them. The only drawback was their appearance.

International society clings resolutely to its old furniture and continues to furnish its rooms in the antique manner. Antique shops multiply daily – proof that the products of modern industrial design are less than ever able to satisfy the demands of customers with the money to buy. We say that the present-day bank manager comes home from his office in a Maybach car and sits down in a Louis Seize salon. Well, where could he sit, so long as he is not offered anything corresponding to his Maybach? Where are the shops in which he could buy furniture *à la* Maybach? The products of the various modern workshops are still far from satisfying such demands. And where are the architects who can build a house *à la* Maybach, supposing the bank director wanted to build one? This is not altogether the architects' fault, however, but is also due to the fact that outside business, bank directors do not like to take risks, that they don't want to bother about the design of a new house and after working hours simply want to take things easy. They *would* buy Maybach houses if they could be offered them.

The present task is to create articles of use which modern man needs. We have working and sports clothes, serviceable sports equipment, serviceable tools, weapons, instruments, ships, cars – but we do not have tables, chairs, furnishing fabrics, etc. to go with them.

When there is nothing more we can take away from an object without destroying it, we have come considerably closer to the goal. A chair is not born with either lion's legs or serpent arms, but nor is it born with nickel-plated steel tubes.

Today society no longer needs furnishings indicating social status, but utilitarian objects. Nor should the latter have any relics of the former attached to them.

We want to furnish our rooms as we consider practical, without stylistic rules and without any kind of compulsion. The utilitarian objects constitute the essential element in the furnishing. Rooms will no longer differ as between Gothic and Empire, but according to the culture of their occupants.

1928 Erich Mendelsohn/Bernhard Hoetger: Synthesis – World Architecture

In a joint publication that was certainly not intended by either of them, the master of architectonic volumes and the sculptor who designed buildings met one another. They came from different worlds. One had sworn allegiance to the big city, had travelled all over the world, knew the horizons of the peoples in West and East. The other lived almost in seclusion in a cavelike house on the moor near Worpswede. World architecture means for the former to combine in one the polar wisdoms of the century; the latter sees his personality as an artist exposed to the cold blast of mechanical tensions. This imaginary dialogue between two essentially different temperaments continues. It is a dialogue between archetypes.

Erich Mendelsohn: Synthesis (Berlin 1928)

The problem of the new world architecture is:
The finiteness of mechanics
plus the infiniteness of life.

The history of America is the history of maximum economic development, the history of the development of the New World on the basis of technology and realistic intelligence. The history of Russia is the history of the unparalleled leap from absolutism and maximum agrarian power to state socialism. The beginning of the history of the New World is development on the basis of technology and intellectual ideas. Hence for both of them, Russia and America, technology is the common soil. It is true that America says: I am the world, I myself am life. Whereas Russia says: I still have to create the world, my life belongs to all men. But both have understood the epoch, impulsively and as though it were a destiny; both are agreed that the communal forms of expression, as they have existed till now, have undergone a fundamental change:

Only the active hand, the active mind has a right to life.
Symbol of the machine, the aeroplane, the splitting of the atom.
God lives only in the deed,
not in faith,
not in reflection.
Art creates only reality.
Art is the highest expression of life,
is life itself.

But: this kind of febrile and over-insistent attitude characteristic of the transition period easily leads into the danger of romanticism. Thus the Russian, technologically speaking still primitive, seeks salvation in the exaggeration

of a form of intelligence alien to him, whereas the technologically highly developed American seeks his in the intensification of a spirituality that is alien to him. Europe will mediate between these two poles of the creative will, America and Russia, provided it remembers itself and retains its overall solidarity, provided it strikes a happy medium, gives expression both to idea and brain, spirit and intelligence. For intelligence regulates our passions – but the human spirit makes the law. Therefore technology ends with man himself. For once technology becomes an end in itself mechanical theory leads to an over-valuation of technical inventions and makes of technology an idol. Therefore no falsification of the human spirit through mechanization. On the contrary, it is the planned subjugation of natural forces to the service of man that first creates the basis for politics and economy. Society, culture, grows on the foundation of the economy. Man, therefore, is not the automated appendage of the machine but its inventor, its master. Only through mastery of his totally altered needs will his vision also become free again for the needs of the mystical elements in his nature that are turned towards the mystery. The hope of the new world has as its signal beacon a magnificent combination: Russia's power of sacrifice.

Vehemence of emotion –
the intuitive,
the impulsively religious element in its nature –

combined with America's unproblematic activeness and energy,
applied at America's high technological level!

Russia and America,
the collective and the individual,
America and Russia,
the earthly and the divine.

This is the problem of the new world architecture:
The finiteness of mechanics
plus the infiniteness of life.

Bernhard Hoetger: World Architecture (Worpswede 1928)

Architecture is unquestionably the most popular of all arts today. The age of the machine, of objectivity, the practice of rendering the construction visible, are captivating recipes and principles, with which the layman can outdo even the expert. Recipes for artistic creation, promulgated by a few, become the treasury of knowledge of the vain. But we ought not to sin against the living spirit, for the spirit of the age seeks in everlasting repetition to transmute itself into matter. The vain striving for objectivity, for beautiful surfaces, for emphasized construction breeds intellect and denies the creative spirit.

Recipes, even architectural recipes, serve the weak, give them the happy possibility of jumping into the circle of creative architects armed with T-square, set square, and intellect. Wise insight and the needs of artistic creation will break through all restrictions imposed by recipes and principles. To appear to be objective does not always mean to be objective. To be objective does not necessarily mean to be artistic, because artistry always presupposes its own objectivity as a matter of course. We want no inhibitions and checks by recipes, we want the free spirit to find its own laws. The creative moment demands not the transparent wall, not the beautiful surface, not construction but synthesis. And this synthesis is not the sum of petty and doubtful details, but the outcome of an intuitive frenzy. Just as creation often demands a gentle shift from meditation to concentration as a prerequisite, so attainment of an eloquent and final form often calls for a detour via superfluity. In 'objective' architecture the vain surface sprawls over a wide area, tolerates neither sculpture nor picture, is self-sufficient at the expense of cosiness. We do not wish to renounce the factors that increase our feeling for life and the world. We want to experience the intoxication of our blood in all things. We do not want to throw the pictures out of our rooms because they are 'irrelevant,' we want rather to draw them into the great joyful rhythm of our house. We want to look at sculpture just as we want to read books, we don't want to ban carpets because they are 'dust traps'. We want the whole wealth of the possible and justified, because it belongs as a necessary factor to our personality. Sculpture and painting will live on in spite of this vain effort at suppression, because in keeping with the times they have set themselves free from architecture to attain a powerful life and content of their own. Cities will change into a shape that restores the sun and movement to the city dweller. This will be the beginning of a new world architecture. What is decisive here will not be the width of the streets, nor the height of the buildings that line them, nor their fronts and outlines, nor their balconies, nor the shapes of their roofs, but solely and alone the creative longing of the citizens. There will be no more corridors and house surfaces, neither in the old nor the new sense, there will be structures that thrust forward and slide back in response to the habits of the occupants, in order to make it possible for them to see and feel the sun again. Roofs will not form an alignment but will lie lower or rise higher as demanded by the desire for roof gardens. Man's longings will be determinant, not the profit motive. We want the individual room, not the factory-made product; we want personality, not norm, not schema, not series, not type. We want no violation of our creative feeling, not even by architecture, we want to live our life. The wealth of the spirit shall glow, all productive possibilities shall blossom, unconcerned about 'objectivity'. Give form to the inner vigour, that cold souls may become warm.

1928　CIAM:
La Sarraz Declaration

One year after the Weissenhof exhibition in Stuttgart, a group of architects –
delegates from various national groups – gathered from 26 to 28 June 1928 at
Château Sarraz in Switzerland. The subject of the meeting was a programme
drawn up in Paris of problems confronting the new architecture. They agreed,
although not without argument, on the standpoints and working methods
proposed by Le Corbusier and Giedion. With a final official declaration CIAM
(Congrès Internationaux d'Architecture Moderne) was considered as founded.
It remained for over thirty years the medium of a world-wide interchange of
ideas. It was the CIAM congresses which brought the objectives of 'town
planning' into perspective.

The undersigned architects, representing the national groups of modern
architects, affirm their unity of viewpoint regarding the fundamental conceptions of architecture and their professional obligations towards society.

They insist particularly on the fact that 'building' is an elementary activity
of man intimately linked with evolution and the development of human life.
The destiny of architecture is to express the orientation of the age. Works of
architecture can spring only from the present time.

They therefore refuse categorically to apply in their working methods
means that may have been able to illustrate past societies; they affirm today
the need for a new conception of architecture that satisfies the spiritual,
intellectual and material demands of present-day life. Conscious of the deep
disturbances of the social structure brought about by machines, they recognize that the transformation of the economic order and of social life inescapably brings with it a corresponding transformation of the architectural
phenomenon.

The intention that brings them together here is to attain the indispensable
and urgent harmonization of the elements involved by replacing architecture
on its true plane, the economic and sociological plane. Thus architecture must
be set free from the sterilizing grip of the academies that are concerned with
preserving the formulas of the past.

Animated by this conviction, they declare themselves members of an
association and will give each other mutual support on the international plane
with a view to realizing their aspirations morally and materially.

I. General Economic System

1. The idea of modern architecture includes the link between the phenomenon
of architecture and that of the general economic system.

2. The idea of 'economic efficiency' does not imply production furnishing
maximum commercial profit, but production demanding a minimum working
effort.

3. The need for maximum economic efficiency is the inevitable result of the impoverished state of the general economy.

4. The most efficient method of production is that which arises from rationalization and standardization. Rationalization and standardization act directly on working methods both in modern architecture (conception) and in the building industry (realization).

5. Rationalization and standardization react in a threefold manner:
(a) they demand of architecture conceptions leading to simplification of working methods on the site and in the factory;
(b) they mean for building firms a reduction in the skilled labour force; they lead to the employment of less specialized labour working under the direction of highly skilled technicians;
(c) they expect from the consumer (that is to say the customer who orders the house in which he will live) a revision of his demands in the direction of a readjustment to the new conditions of social life. Such a revision will be manifested in the reduction of certain individual needs henceforth devoid of real justification; the benefits of this reduction will foster the maximum satisfaction of the needs of the greatest number, which are at present restricted.

6. Following the dissolution of the guilds, the collapse of the class of skilled craftsmen is an accomplished fact. The inescapable consequence of the development of the machine has led to industrial methods of production different from and often opposed to those of the craftsmen. Until recently, thanks to the teaching of the academies, the architectural conception has been inspired chiefly by the methods of craftsmen and not by the new industrial methods. This contradiction explains the profound disorganization of the art of building.

7. It is urgently necessary for architecture, abandoning the outmoded conceptions connected with the class of craftsmen, henceforth to rely upon the present realities of industrial technology, even though such an attitude must perforce lead to products fundamentally different from those of past epochs.

II. Town Planning

1. Town planning is the organization of the functions of collective life; it extends over both the urban agglomerations and the countryside. Town planning is the organization of life in all regions.

Urbanization cannot be conditioned by the claims of a pre-existent aestheticism: its essence is of a functional order.

2. This order includes three functions: (a) dwelling, (b) producing, (c) relaxation (the maintenance of the species).

Its essential objects are: (a) division of the soil, (b) organization of traffic, (c) legislation.

3. The relationships between the inhabited areas, the cultivated areas (including sports) and the traffic areas are dictated by the economic and social environment. The fixing of population densities establishes the indispensable classification.

The chaotic division of land, resulting from sales, speculations, inheritances, must be abolished by a collective and methodical land policy.

This redistribution of the land, the indispensable preliminary basis for any town planning, must include the just division between the owners and the community of the *unearned increment* resulting from works of joint interest.

4. Traffic control must take in all the functions of collective life. The growing intensity of these vital functions, always checked against a reading of statistics, demonstrates the supreme importance of the traffic phenomenon.

5. Present-day technical facilities, which are constantly growing, are the very key to town planning. They imply and offer a total transformation of existing legislation; this transformation must run parallel with technical progress.

III. Architecture and public opinion

1. It is essential today for architects to exercise an influence on public opinion by informing the public of the fundamentals of the new architecture. Through the baneful effects of academic teaching, opinion has strayed into an erroneous conception of the dwelling. The true problems of the dwelling have been pushed back behind entirely artificial sentimental conceptions. The problem of the house is not posed.

Clients, whose demands are motivated by numerous factors that have nothing to do with the real problem of housing, are generally very bad at formulating their wishes. Opinion has gone astray. Thus the architect satisfies the normal prerequisites of housing only poorly. This inefficiency involves the country in an immense expense that is a total loss. The tradition is created of the expensive house, the building of which deprives a large part of the population of healthy living quarters.

2. Through educational work carried out in schools, a body of fundamental truths could be established forming the basis for a domestic science (for example: the general economy of the dwelling, the principles of property and its moral significance, the effects of sunlight, the ill effects of darkness, essential hygiene, rationalization of household economics, the use of mechanical devices in domestic life, etc.)

3. The effect of such an education would be to bring up generations with a healthy and rational conception of the house. These generations (the

architect's future clients) would be capable of correctly stating the problems of housing.

IV. Architecture and its relations with the State

1. Modern architects having the firm intention of working according to the new principles can only regard the official academies and their methods tending towards aestheticism and formalism as institutions standing in the way of progress.

2. These academies, by definition and by function, are the guardians of the past. They have established dogmas of architecture based on the practical and aesthetic methods of historical periods. Academies vitiate the architect's vocation at its very origin. Their point of view is erroneous and its consequences are erroneous.

3. In order to guarantee the country's prosperity, therefore, States must tear the teaching of architecture out of the grip of the academies. The past teaches us precisely that nothing remains, that everything evolves and that progress constantly advances.

4. States, henceforth withdrawing their confidence from the academies, must revise the methods of teaching architecture and concern themselves with this question as they concern themselves with all those questions whose object is to endow the country with the most productive and most advanced systems of organization.

5. Academicism causes States to spend considerable sums on the erection of monumental buildings, contrary to the efficient utilization of resources, making a display of outmoded luxury at the expense of the most urgent tasks of town planning and housing.

6. Within the same order of ideas, all the prescriptions of the State which, in one form or another, tend to influence architecture by giving it a purely aesthetic direction are an obstacle to its development and must be vigorously combated.

7. Architecture's new attitude, according to which it aims of its own volition to re-situate itself within economic reality, renders all claim to official patronage superfluous.

8. If States were to adopt an attitude opposite to their present one they would bring about a veritable architectural renaissance that would take its place quite naturally within the general orientation of the country's economic and social development.

28 June 1928

The Declaration was signed by the following architects:

H. P. Berlage, The Hague
V. Bourgeois, Brussels
P. Chareau, Paris
J. Frank, Vienna
G. Guevrekian, Paris
M. E. Haefeli, Zürich
H. Häring, Berlin
A. Höchel, Geneva
H. Hoste, St Michiels
P. Jeanneret, Paris
Le Corbusier, Paris
A. Lurçat, Paris

E. May, Frankfurt a/M.
A. G. Mercadal, Madrid
Hannes Meyer, Bauhaus Dessau
W. M. Moser, Zürich
E. C. Rava, Milan
G. Rietveld, Utrecht
A. Sartoris, Turin
Hans Schmidt, Basle
Mart Stam, Rotterdam
R. Steiger, Zürich
H. R. von der Mühll, Lausanne
Juan de Zavala, Madrid

DE 8?

DE 8 IS de critische reactie op de architectonische vormgeving van dezen dag.

DE 8 IS realist in zijn streven naar onmiddellijke resultaten.

DE 8 IS idealist in zijn geloof aan een inte... ...tureele coöperatie.

DE 8 IS opportunist uit maatschappelij...

DE 8 IS noch voor noch tegen groepen... ...noc tegen richtingen.

DE 8 IS slechts voor feiten.

DE 8 ZEGT het is niet uitgesl... ...te bo het ware beter voo... ...lijk t doelmatig, dan pa... ...ctuur ken voor slechte p... ...en.

DE 8 W I L zich ondergeschikt m... ...cht.

DE 8 W I L geen weelde archit... ...de vormenwellust van... ...erde

DE 8 W I L rationeel zijn in de... ...n, d.w moet wijken voor... ...van d

DE 8 W I L streven naar een... ...lijke voor den moderne... ...De a mode is een goed... ...g zich ken tot een luxe e... ...verle

DE 8 STRIJDT uitsluite... ...ingen

DE 8 WERKT meer vo... ... SCHAP da... ...T.

DE 8 STREEFT naar een plaats in de samenleving als:

BEELDEND BEDRIJFS-ORGANISATOR

DE 8 IS A-AESTHETISCH

DE 8 IS A-DRAMATISCH

DE 8 IS A-ROMANTISCH

DE 8 IS RESULTANTE   DE 8 IS A-KUBISTISCH

Correspondentie-Adres, Architectenkern „de 8", B. Merkelbach, Arch., Noorderstraat 72, Amsterdam. Tel. 33072

1928 A
B
C demands the dictatorship of the machine

Hans Schmidt, Basle, and Mart Stam, Rotterdam, edited the periodical *ABC –
Beiträge zum Bauen* (Contributions Towards Building) which appeared in Basle.
The demand for the dictatorship of the machine, taken from No.4, Vol.2, is
closely connected with the ideas of Hannes Meyer, who in 1928 took over from
Walter Gropius as director of the Dessau Bauhaus.

The   is neither the coming paradise in which technology will fulfil all
machine   our wishes – nor the approaching hell in which all human
development will be destroyed –

The   is nothing more than the inexorable dictator of the possibilities
machine   and tasks common to all our lives.

But we are still in a state of becoming, of transition. The machine has become
the servant of a bourgeois individualist culture born of the Renaissance. Just
as the servant is paid and despised by the same master, so the machine is
simultaneously used by the citizen and damned by his intellectual court, his
artists, scholars and philosophers. The machine is not a servant, however, but
a dictator – it dictates how we are to think and what we have to understand.
As leader of the masses, who are inescapably bound up with it, it demands
more insistently every year the transformation of our economy, our culture.
It permits no pause for breath in the armchair of philosophy, no compromise
with pacifist phrases. It grants us no prospect of an agreed peace, no aesthetic
distance from the demands of life. Reality shows us how far we have already
gone today in obeying the dictates of the machine: we have sacrificed handicrafts to it, we are in the process of offering up the peasantry to it. We have
had to allow it to provide our most important means of travel and the basis
for our great industries. Under its pressure we have evolved the new method
of mass-production. Because of it we have had to place greater and greater
organizational powers in the hands of the State and even to internationalize
our most sacred national goods.

We have taken the first step:

the transition from an individualistically producing society held together
ideally by the concepts of the national State and a racially delimited religious
outlook, to a capitalistically producing society *materially* organized in response to the need for industrialization and the international exchange of
goods. But our thinking, the thinking of our professional romantics and life-
titivators, has not followed even this step. They have ceased to understand

elemental, vital facts because they think exclusively in terms of morality and aesthetics. And because they fear the worst for the future of our ideal goods, namely, that they themselves will be out of work, sheer idealism makes them either become the bodyguard of reaction or take flight into sectarianism.

We have to take the second step:

the transition from a society that is *compelled* to produce collectively but is still individualistically orientated to a society that *consciously* thinks and works collectively. Empty phrases? Empty phrases to the ears of bourgeois armchair sceptics – implacable necessity to the masses who have today been thrust out to the edge of survival. They are empty phrases if we believe we could make bourgeois idealistic thinking the basis for constructing a lucid, rational system of production – if we believe our Sunday-afternoon-walk culture only needs to be reduced in price a little – if we believe we could dodge the most important and decisive struggle of the immediate future by making a cheap peace. What is demanded of us is in the first place the liberation and transformation of our thinking. Everywhere necessities are forcing action – what is missing is correct thinking on the part of those destined to act and to lead – for elemental thinking has been suffocated by the empty phrases and illusions of reaction.

1928 Hannes Meyer: Building

In 1928 Hannes Meyer (b.1889 in Basle, d.1954 in Crocifisso di Savosa, Switzerland) was appointed head of the Bauhaus in Dessau. Walter Gropius retired at the beginning of February 1928 and recommended him as his successor. The same month Meyer outlined before representatives of the students his programme, which was aimed essentially at a closer combination of teaching and work in the Bauhaus with life. 'Do we wish to take our direction from the needs of the outer world . . . or do we want to be an island which admittedly leads to a broadening of the personality, but whose positive productivity is questionable?' His thesis 'building' was published in *bauhaus* Year 2, No.4.

building

all things in this world are a product of the formula: (function times economy).

all these things are, therefore, not works of art:
all art is composition and, hence, is unsuited to achieve goals.
all life is function and is therefore unartistic.
the idea of the 'composition of a harbour' is hilarious!
but how is a town plan designed? or a plan of a dwelling? composition or function? art or life?????
building is a biological process. building is not an aesthetic process.
in its design the new dwelling becomes not only a 'machine for living', but also a biological apparatus serving the needs of body and mind.
the new age provides new building materials for the new way of building houses:

reinforced concrete	aluminium	ripolin
synthetic rubber	euböolith	viscose
synthetic leather	plywood	asbestos concrete
porous concrete	hard rubber	bitumen
woodmetal	torfoleum	canvas
wire-mesh glass	silicon steel	asbestos
pressed cork	cold glue	acetone
synthetic resin	cellular concrete	casein
synthetic horn	rolled glass	trolite
synthetic wood	xelotect	tombac

we organize these building materials into a constructive whole based on economic principles. thus the individual shape, the body of the structure, the colour of the material and the surface texture evolve by themselves and are determined by life. (snugness and prestige are not leitmotifs for dwelling construction.) (the first depends on the human heart and not on the walls of a room . . .) (the second manifests itself in the manner of the host and not by his persian carpet!)

bauen

alle dinge dieser welt sind ein produkt der formel: (funktion mal ökonomie)

alle diese dinge sind daher keine kunstwerke:
alle kunst ist komposition und mithin zweckwidrig.
alles leben ist funktion und daher unkünstlerisch.
die idee der „komposition eines seehafens" scheint zwerchfellerschütternd!
jedoch wie ersteht der entwurf eines stadtplanes? oder eines wohnplanes? komposition oder funktion?
kunst oder leben? ? ? ? ?
bauen ist ein biologischer vorgang. bauen ist kein aesthetischer prozeß. elementar gestaltet wird das neue wohn-
haus nicht nur eine wohnmaschinerie, sondern ein biologischer apparat für seelische und körperliche
bedürfnisse. — die neue zeit stellt dem neuen hausbau ihre neuen baustoffe zur verfügung:

stahlbeton	drahtglas	aluminium	si-stahl	ripolin	asbest
kunstgummi	preßkork	euböolith	kaltleim	viscose	azeton
kunstleder	kunstharz	sperrholz	gasbeton	eternit	casein
zell-beton	kunsthorn	kautschuk	rollglas	goudron	trolit
woodmetall	kunstholz	torfoleum	xelotekt	kanevas	tombak

diese bauelemente organisieren wir nach ökonomischen grundsätzen zu einer konstruktiven einheit. so
erstehen selbsttätig und vom leben bedingt die einzelform, der gebäudekörper, die materialfarbe und die
oberflächenstruktur. (gemütlichkeit und repräsentation sind keine leitmotive des wohnungsbaues.)
(die erste hängt am menschenherzen und nicht an der zimmerwand. . . .)
(die zweite prägt die haltung des gastgebers und nicht sein perserteppich!)
architektur als „affektleistung des künstlers" ist ohne daseinsberechtigung.
architektur als „fortführung der bautradition" ist baugeschichtlich treiben.

diese funktionell-biologische auffassung des bauens als einer gestaltung des lebensprozesses führt mit
folgerichtigkeit zur reinen konstruktion: diese konstruktive formenwelt kennt kein vaterland. sie ist der
ausdruck internationaler baugesinnung. internationalität ist ein vorzug der epoche. **die reine konstruktion
ist grundlage und kennzeichen der neuen formenwelt.**

1. geschlechtsleben	4. gartenkultur	7. wohnhygiene	10. erwärmung
2. schlafgewohnheit	5. körperpflege	8. autowartung	11. besonnung
3. kleintierhaltung	6. wetterschutz	9. kochbetrieb	12. bedienung

solche forderungen sind die ausschließlichen motive des wohnungsbaues. wir untersuchen den ablauf des
tageslebens jedes hausbewohners, und dieses ergibt das funktionsdiagramm für vater, mutter, kind,
kleinkind und mitmenschen. wir erforschen die beziehungen des hauses und seiner insassen zum fremden:
postbote, passant, besucher, nachbar, einbrecher, kaminfeger, wäscherin, polizist, arzt, aufwartefrau, spiel-
kamerad, gaseinzüger, handwerker, krankenpfleger, bote. wir erforschen die menschlichen und die
tierischen beziehungen zum garten, und die wechselwirkungen zwischen menschen, haustieren und haus-
insekten. wir ermitteln die jahresschwankungen der bodentemperatur, und wir berechnen danach den
wärmeverlust der fußböden und die tiefe der fundamentsohlen. — der geologische befund des haus-

architecture as 'an emotional act of the artist' has no justification.
architecture as 'a continuation of the traditions of building' means being carried along by the history of architecture.
this functional, biological interpretation of architecture as giving shape to the functions of life, logically leads to pure construction: this world of constructive forms knows no native country. it is the expression of an international attitude in architecture. internationality is a privilege of the period. **pure construction is the basis and the characteristic of the new world of forms.**

1. sex life	5. personal hygiene	9. cooking
2. sleeping habits	6. weather protection	10. heating
3. pets	7. hygiene in the home	11. exposure to the sun
4. gardening	8. car maintenance	12. service

these are the only motives when building a house. we examine the daily routine of everyone who lives in the house and this gives us the function-diagram for the father, the mother, the child, the baby and the other occupants. we explore the relationships of the house and its occupants to the world outside: postman, passer-by, visitor, neighbour, burglar, chimney-sweep, washerwoman, policeman, doctor, charwoman, playmate, gas inspector, tradesman, nurse, and messenger boy, we explore the relationships of human beings and animals to the garden, and the interrelationships between human beings, pets, and domestic insects. we determine the annual fluctuations in the temperature of the ground and from that calculate the heat loss of the floor and the resulting depth required for the foundation blocks. the geological nature of the soil informs us about its capillary capability and determines whether water will naturally drain away or whether drains are required. we calculate the angle of the sun's incidence during the course of the year according to the latitude of the site. with that information we determine the size of the shadow cast by the house on the garden and the amount of sun admitted by the window into the bedroom. we estimate the amount of daylight available for interior working areas. we compare the heat conductivity of the outside walls with the humidity of the air outside the house. we already know about the circulation of air in a heated room. the visual and acoustical relationships to neighbouring dwellings are most carefully considered. knowing the atavistic inclinations of the future inhabitants with respect to the kind of wood finish we can offer, we select the interior finish for the standardized, prefabricated dwelling accordingly: marble-grained pine, austere poplar, exotic okumé or silky maple. colour to us is merely a means for intentional psychological influence or a means of orientation. colour is never a false copy of various kinds of material. we loathe variegated colour. we consider paint to be a protective coating. where we think colour to be psychically indispensable, we include in our calculation the amount of light reflection it offers. we avoid using a purely white finish on the house. we consider the body of the house to be an accumulator of the sun's warmth . . .

the new house is a prefabricated building for site assembly; as such it is an industrial product and the work of a variety of specialists: economists, statisticians, hygienists, climatologists, industrial engineers, standardization experts, heating engineers . . . and the architect? . . . he was an artist and now becomes a specialist in organization!

the new house is a social enterprise. it frees the building industry from partial seasonal unemployment and from the odium of unemployment relief work. by rationalized housekeeping methods it saves the housewife from household slavery, and by rationalized gardening methods it protects the householder from the dilettantism of the small gardener. it is primarily a social enterprise because it is – like every government standard – the standardized, industrial product of a nameless community of inventors.

the new housing project as a whole is to be the ultimate aim of public welfare and as such is an intentionally organized, public-spirited project in which collective and individual energies are merged in a public-spiritedness based on an integral, co-operative foundation. the modernness of such an estate does not consist of a flat roof and a horizontal-vertical arrangement of the façade, but rather of its direct relationship to human existence. in it we have given thoughtful consideration to the tensions of the individual, the sexes, the neighbourhood and the community, as well as to geophysical relationships.

building   is the deliberate organization of the processes of life.

building   as a technical process is therefore only one part of the whole process. the functional diagram and the economic programme are the determining principles of the building project.

building   is no longer an individual task for the realization of architectural ambitions.

building   is the communal effort of craftsmen and inventors. only he who, as a master in the working community of others, masters life itself . . . is a master builder.

building   then grows from being an individual affair of individuals (promoted by unemployment and the housing shortage) into a collective affair of the whole nation.

building   is nothing but organization:
social, technical, economic, psychological organization.

1929   El Lissitzky:
Ideological superstructure

After long residence in Germany and Switzerland, El (Eleazar Markovich)
Lissitzky (b.1890 in the province of Smolensk, d.1941 in Moscow) returned to
Russia. He was almost certainly the first to make the Constructivist ideas of 1920
known in Germany. At the Düsseldorf Congress of Progressive Artists in 1922 he
met artistic revolutionaries from all over Europe. He worked with Mies van der
Rohe in Berlin and with van Doesburg in Paris and showed his 'Proun'
exhibition in many places. Enriched by the sum total of all these encounters,
Lissitzky returned in 1928 to Moscow, in order there to push through a
'reconstruction' in his sense against an already active opposition.

We shall present here a few sections of a life process which, having been first
brought into existence by the Revolution, is a bare 5 years old. During this
time the high demands made by the cultural revolution have taken root in the
feelings and consciousness of our new generation of architects. It has become
clear to our architect that through his work he is playing an active part in
building the new world. To use an artist's work has no value *per se*, no purpose of its own, no beauty of its own; it receives all this solely from its relation
to the community. In the creation of every great work the architect's part is
visible and the community's part latent. The artist, the creator, invents
nothing that falls into his lap from the sky. Therefore we understand by
'reconstruction' the overcoming of the unclear, the 'mysterious' and chaotic.

In our architecture, as in our whole life, we are striving to create a social
order, that is to say, to raise the instinctual into consciousness.

The ideological superstructure protects and guarantees the work. As the
substructure for the renewal that we must carry out in architecture, we named
at the beginning the social economic reconstruction. It is the unequivocal
starting point, but it would be a mistake to explain the interconnexions so
simply. Life, organic growth, is a dialectical process that simultaneously
asserts yes (plus) and no (minus). Everything that comes into being is a part of
the process of social life, the result of particular facts, and itself exercises an
influence on the aims that come into being in their turn. On the basis of what
has come into being there is formed an ideology, a way of looking at things,
there are formed interpretation and interrelationships, which exercise a
further influence on what is coming into being. We may trace this dialectical
process in the development of our architects.

1. Destruction of the traditional. Material production is paralysed throughout
the country. The longing for a super-production. The first studio dreams. An
ideology is formed containing two demands that are fundamental to further
development: element and invention. A work that is to be in keeping with our
age must contain within it an invention. Our age demands creations arising
out of elemental forms (geometry). War has been declared on the aesthetic of

chaos. An order that has entered fully into consciousness is called for.

2. The start of rebuilding. First in industry and production. Concrete problems demand solution. But the new generation has grown up in a period without architecture, has inadequate practical experience, little authority, and has not yet become an academy. In the struggle for building contracts its ideology has turned to the primary utilitarian, the nakedly functional. The slogan is: 'Constructivism', 'Functionalism'. An equals sign has been placed between engineer and architect . . .

3. The first reconstruction period demands a concentration of forces from the sphere of the socio-economic revolution to bring about a deepening of the cultural revolution. In the total complex of a culture, physical, psychological and emotional factors are inseparable.

Art is acknowledged in its capacity to order, organize, and activate consciousness by charging it with emotional energy. Architecture is considered the leading art and the attention of the public is directed towards it. Architectural questions become mass questions. The studio dreams of the beginning lose their individual character and receive a solid social foundation. Once again the 'Utilitarians' are opposed by the 'Formalists'. The latter assert that architecture is not covered by the concept of 'engineering'. To solve the utilitarian task, to construct a volume that functions correctly for the purpose, is only one part of the problem. The second part is to organize the materials correctly, to solve the constructive problem. A work of architecture comes into being only when the whole thing springs to life as a spatial idea, as a form that exercises a definite effect on our psyche. To do this it is not enough to be a modern man; it is necessary for the architect to possess a complete mastery of the expressive means of architecture.

Thus we can summarize these three periods even more briefly:
(a) Denial of art as merely an emotional, individual affair carried on in romantic isolation.
(b) 'Objective' creation in the silent hope that the resulting product will eventually be looked upon as a work of art.
(c) Conscious and purposeful creation of an architecture that will exercise a closed artistic effect on an objective, scientific basis that has been worked out in advance.

This architecture will actively raise the general standard of living.

This is the dialectic of our development, which reaches affirmation through denial; it has melted down the old iron and annealed the new steel.

1930　Ludwig Mies van der Rohe: The new era

In the closing words of his address at the congress of the Deutscher Werkbund in Vienna in 1930 Mies van der Rohe made himself the resolute spokesman for the 'spiritual in architecture'. He saw the path of industrialized building, for which he had appealed in 1924, blocked by misunderstanding. The appealer has become a warner. In prophetic anticipation he foresees that technical progress will bring with it a loss of the meaning of building. Mies van der Rohe speaks of the 'value-blind' progress of events, which will lead to the elimination of meaning and hence to a lack of standards and to chaos in the establishment of values.

The new era is a fact; it exists entirely independently of whether we say 'yes' or 'no' to it. But it is neither better nor worse than any other era. It is a pure datum and in itself neutral as to value. Therefore I shall not spend long trying to elucidate the new era, to demonstrate its links and lay bare its supporting structure.

Let us also not overestimate the question of mechanization, standardization and normalization.

And let us accept the changed economic and social conditions as fact.

All these things go their destined way, blind to values.

The decisive thing is which of these given facts we choose to emphasize. This is where spiritual problems begin.

What matters is not 'what' but only 'how'.

That we produce goods and by what means we manufacture them means nothing, spiritually speaking.

Whether we build high or low, with steel and glass, tells us nothing about the value of the building.

Whether in town planning we aim at centralization or decentralization is a practical question, not one of value.

But precisely the question of value is decisive.

We have to establish new values, to demonstrate ultimate aims, in order to acquire criteria.

For the meaning and right of every age, including our own, consists solely in providing the spirit with the necessary prerequisites for its existence.

1931 Frank Lloyd Wright: Young architecture (excerpt)

The excerpt reproduced here under the heading 'Young Architecture' is taken from one of the lectures delivered by Wright at the Chicago Art Institute in 1931. This lecture was addressed 'To the young man in architecture' and closes with fourteen pieces of advice to future architects: Forget the architectures of the world – beware of schools of architecture – go to the building sites – get used to asking questions and analysing – think in terms of simple things – avoid like poison the American idea of 'quick returns' – take plenty of time and go as far away as possible from home – under no circumstances take part in an architectural competition. The following are a few sentences from this guide to young architects.

Yes, modern architecture is young architecture – the joy of youth must bring it. The love of youth, eternal youth must develop and keep it. You must see this architecture as wise, but not so much wise as sensible and wistful – nor any more scientific than sentient, nor so much resembling a flying machine as a masterpiece of the imagination.

Oh yes, young man; consider well that a house is a machine in which to live, but by the same token a heart is a suction pump. Sentient man begins where that concept of the heart ends.

Consider well that a house is a machine in which to live but architecture begins where that concept of the house ends. All life is machinery in a rudimentary sense, and yet machinery is the life of nothing. Machinery is machinery only because of life. It is better for you to proceed from the generals to the particulars. So do not rationalize from machinery to life. Why not think from life to machines? The utensil, the weapon, the automaton – all are *appliances*. The song, the masterpiece, the edifice are a warm outpouring of the heart of man – human delight in life triumphant: we glimpse the infinite.

That glimpse or vision is what makes art a matter of inner experience, therefore sacred, and no less but rather more individual in this age, I assure you, than ever before . . .

Lack of appreciation of the difference between the appliance and life is to blame for the choicest pseudo-classic horrors in America. And yet our more successful 'modern' architects are still busy applying brick or stone envelopes to steel frames in the great American cities. Instead of fundamentally correcting this error, shall any superficial aesthetic disguised as new enable this same lack of appreciation of the principles of architecture to punish us again this time with a machinery abstract which will be used as an appliance of the appliance of another cycle of thirty years? If so as between architecture as sentimental appliance and architecture as mechanical appliance or even the aesthetic abstract itself as an architectural appliance, it would be better for America were you to choose architecture as the mechanical appliance. But then, organic architecture would have to keep on in a little world of its own. In this world of its own the hard line and the bare upright plane in unimaginative contours of the box both have a place, just as the carpet has a place on the floor, but the creed of the naked stilt, as a stilt, has no place. The horizontal plane gripping all to earth comes into organic architecture to complete the sense of forms that do not 'box up' contents but imaginatively express space. This is modern.

In organic architecture the hard straight line breaks to the dotted line where stark necessity ends and thus allows appropriate rhythm to enter in order to leave suggestion its proper values. This is modern.

In organic architecture, any conception of any building as a building begins at the beginning and goes *forward* to incidental expression as a picture and does not begin with some incidental expression as a picture and go groping *backward*. This is modern.

Eye-weary of reiterated bald commonplaces wherein light is rejected from blank surfaces or fallen dismally into holes cut in them, organic architecture brings the man once more face to face with nature's play of shade and depth of shadow seeing fresh vistas of native creative human thought and native feeling presented to his imagination for consideration. This is modern.

The sense of interior space as a reality in organic architecture co-ordinates with the enlarged means of modern materials. The building is now found in this sense of interior space; the enclosure is no longer found in terms of mere roof or walls but as 'screened' space. This reality is modern.

In true modern architecture, therefore, the sense of surface and mass disappears in light, or fabrications that combine it with strength. And this fabrication is no less the expression of principle as power-directed-toward-purpose than may be seen in any modern appliance or utensil machine. But modern architecture affirms the higher human sensibility of the sunlit space. Organic buildings are the strength and lightness of the spiders' spinning, buildings qualified by light, bred by native character to environment – married to the ground. That is modern!

1932 Hugo Häring:
The house as an organic structure (excerpt)

In 1928, as representative of the Berlin architects' association Der Ring, whose
secretary he was, Hugo Häring took part in the founding of CIAM at Château
Sarraz. It there proved that the initiators of the congress, Le Corbusier and
Siegfried Giedion, could not accept the concept of 'new building' presented by
Häring. There is no French word exactly equivalent to 'building'. Yet for
Häring architecture and building are fundamentally different. Building meant
for him: to give physical shape to the substance of a task. Form is in this sense
result, not starting point. The important thing is to see the house as an organ
that first acquires its essential shape in the actual process of creation.

It still seems to many people inconceivable that a house too may be evolved
entirely as an 'organic structure', that it may be 'bred' out of the 'form arising
out of work performance', in other words that the house may be looked upon
as 'man's second skin' and hence as a bodily organ. And yet this development
seems inescapable. A new technology, working with light constructions,
elastic and malleable building materials, will no longer demand a rectangular
house, but permit or put into effect all shapes that make the house into a
'housing organ'. The gradual structural shift from the geometrical to the
organic, which is taking place throughout our whole spiritual life and to some
extent has already taken place, has made the form of work performance mobile as opposed to geometrical. The need to create form constantly leads the
artist to experiment with styles, repeatedly leads him, in the interest of expression, to spread shapes over objects – whereas the form arising out of work
performance leads to every object receiving and retaining its own essential
shape. The artist stands in the most essential contradiction to the form of
work performance so long as he refuses to give up his individuality; for in
operating with the form arising out of work performance the artist is no longer
concerned with the expression of his own individuality but with the expression
of the essence of as perfect as possible a utilitarian object. All 'individuals' –
and the stronger they are as personalities, and at times the louder they are, the
more this applies – are an obstacle in the path of development, and in fact
progress takes place in spite of them. But nor does progress take place without
them, without individuals, artists and strong personalities. There remains an
essential difference between the architect and the engineer. The work of the
engineer has as its goal merely the performance of material work within the
limits or in the domain of economic effects. That the result frequently contains other expressive values as well is a side-effect, a subsidiary phenomenon
of his work. The architect, on the other hand, creates a *Gestalt*, a total form,
a work of spiritual vitality and fulfilment, an object that belongs to and serves
an idea, a higher culture.

This work begins where the engineer, the technologist, leaves off; it begins when the work is given life. Life is not given to the work by fashioning the object, the building, according to a viewpoint alien to it, but by awakening, fostering, and cultivating the essential form enclosed within it.

1932   R. Buckminster Fuller: Universal architecture

Richard Buckminster Fuller (b.1895 in Milton, Massachusetts) developed in 1927 his 'Dymaxion House', a dwelling machine in which, as its name implies, dynamism was to be combined with maximum efficiency. This combination of technical and civilizing tendencies – in 1932–3 the 'Dymaxion Automobile' developed out of it – made the outsider well known in Europe as well. His theoretical writings of this period are pretty unintelligible. Together with the Structural Study Associates (SSA), whose members remained anonymous, Fuller developed the idea of a universal architecture. It is based on a highly individual interpretation of life: the ideal can be pictorially reproduced.

EXTRACTS FROM 'UNIVERSAL CONDITIONS' OF STRUCTURAL STUDY ASSOCIATES

ORGANIZATIONS PLUS AND MINUS. THE SSA. A PLUS UNION

Official, or semi-official, exploitation and protective associations in architecture, real estate, business, etc., whose professional opportunist management, effete counterpart of labour, boss, or vice racketeer, representative, not of the dominant ideals, or progressive standards of the group whom they have organized, but of the negative residuary quantums of fear, bad faith, jealousy, covetousness, non-self-confidence, and laziness, hold their prestige, and job, so long as they can, first – aggravate their membership's fear of the emergencies caused by progressive industry's threat to static exploitation, and secondly by sustaining an aesthetic or ethic leech-hold upon pioneering productivity. Such associations have constituted a dominant obstacle to universal architecture – and conversely the high potential of current economic stress.

It is worthy of note that the SSA represents a group mechanically cohesive through a positive creative and progressive urge, no personal names being identified with the work, members being designated only by numbers, as compared to designers' associations boastfully exploiting past records of members. Self-effacing, and service-minded, somewhat after the manner of the Ford planning department, they concern themselves not alone with the final structure, to be reproduced in quantity, but also with the complete ramifications of the industry, from elemental source to the site; and, thereafter, throughout service and replacement cycles, calling even for searching consideration of contiguous sociologic development and its potentials for further growth, through design.

The group, forming an abstract association, held together only through 'good faith' and a singleness of purpose, deals only in intercourse of ideas, but cannot buy or sell. (The writer has assigned all his sixty-two patent ideas to the trusteeship of the SSA.) All ideas developed by the group will be protected to prevent monopolies in industrial design, but never to paternalize selfish advancement – or to enjoin progress.

I. SCIENCE

The word 'science' as defined by Eddington, and generally agreed to by Pasadena group scientists, is extraordinarily simple – to wit:

'Science is the attempt (continuity or time word) to set in order the facts of experience.' To which we add that: science is the resultant of intellectual activity which is essentially:

'Selection' an individual phenomena, time controlling, and the human phenomena's unique survival tool – intellect is sole guide to 'Universal Architecture', which is humanity's supreme survival gesture. Universal Architecture scientific antidote for war.

STRUCTURE=SCIENTIFIC ARTICULATION

Universal requirements of structure provide for scientific survival and development of human phenomena, in following sequence:

1. OPPOSITION TO EXTERNAL DESTRUCTIVE FORCES, via spatial control against:
   > earthquake
   > flood
   > gale
   > tornado
   > pestilence
   > marauders
   > fire
   > gases
   > selfishness (Politics, Business, Materialism)

2. OPPOSITION OF INTERNAL DESTRUCTIVE FORCES, via spatial control for:
   a. nerve shock proofing
      1. visual
      2. oral
      3. textural
      4. olfactoral
   b. fatigue proofing (human robotism, drudgery).
   c. repression proofing (don't proofing, fear mechanical inadequacy developed by accidents, arbitrary cellular limits of activity), (negative partitioning).

3. PROVISION FOR UNSELFCONSCIOUS PERFORMANCE ON INEVITABLE MECHANICAL ROUTINE
   a. fuelling (eating), (metabolism).
   b. sleeping (muscular, nerve and cellular re-alignment).

c. refusing (internal, i.e., intestinal, etc.; external, i.e., bathing or pore cleansing; mental, i.e., elimination by empirical dynamics; circulatory, i.e., atmospheric control).

4. DEVELOPMENT REQUIREMENTS OF GROWTH PHENOMENA, require mechanical provision for:
   a. selective awareness of universal progressions
      1. History – News – Forecasts (Library-Radio-Television, etc.)
      2. Supply and Demand
      3. Dynamics
   b. adequate mechanics of articulation (prosaic or harmonic) conversation, i.e., communication, direct or indirect, oral, visual or textural, (this includes necessity of transportation) and bespeaks any and all means of crystallization of universal progress.

II. ART

ART = net resultant of momentarily (time fix) dominant articulability of ego's cosmic sense.

1. Time
Scientific concept indicates one dimension only, i.e. – TIME DIMENSION – indicating 'how far' from the centre out. This dimension geometrically articulatable by any one of infinity of coincident radii of a sphere. (Which accounts for coincidence of 'the infinity of unity' with 'the infinity of multiplicity'.)

'Raising' an abstract indicator, or number, to any 'power', or taking any 'root' of it, now graphable by spheroidal volume increase, or decrease, respectively, through proportionate radial increase, or decrease; – there being an infinity of potential perpendiculars to surface of sphere identical to radii, which fulfils Euclid's requirement for additional dimensional characteristics, non-graphable above 3 in Euclid's suppositional cubistic universe, but spheroidally graphable as indicated by simple mathematics, wherefor:

Essence of design = time control.

Essence of universal discourse should be time language or language of continuity (discarding such words as 'fundamental' or basic).

2. Space
Universal problem of architecture is to compass space (space being mathematically convertible to time via the abstraction of angularity).

Problem is, subsequently, to control the space compassed; and subsequently to develop selective control of compassed space, which control will allow of ever variable complementary harmonic awareness of any and all sense-organizations to be sheltered within the compassed space.

3. *Harmony*

We can only be aware of structure via its harmonic continuity reaction (minor or major mode, damn or please) upon one or more of our four senses – visual, oral, textural, olfactoral. Só that each unit of structure should be checked as to its neutral aspect in relation to these four senses, and the ability, thereafter, should be mechanically provided, to impose an infinity of mutable, selective sense-limited, harmonic progressions thereon, consistent with de-selfing trend of harmony, from direct personality limit to abstract infinity.

III. INDUSTRY

By 'ideal' we mean the latest sensation of refinement towards perfection along any one time line, and by 'standard' the group ideal. The 'standard' being graphed by the most encompassing sphere of our awareness terminating the conscious exterior limits of all our radionic time lines of experience.

By 'industry' we mean the phenomena of scientific human-effort-co-ordination of three or more beings, which, through selected activity of the two-or-more beings, made possible by the third being, in whom the two-or-more divided-activity-performers have faith that: he truly has divided the effort; and will co-ordinate that effort, to the end that: mutually profitable resultant compositions are obtained, within a reasonable time limit, beyond the physical ability of any being, or group of beings, non-mentally co-ordinated, to obtain, within all time. Industry can only concern itself with reproduction of those designs which adequately satisfy the 'standard', and are reproduceable in a quantity directly proportionable to their timeliness and adequacy; in relation to which, industrial satisfaction, 'standards' improve (include and refine), and without which satisfaction standards cannot improve – such is the human progress responsibility of reproductive design, being based on our philosophic interpretation of LIFE, to wit, that that which is ideal enough becomes reproducible in its own image, be it a baby, rose, or bicycle.

Science + Art + Industry = Universal Architecture

ESSENTIAL PHILOSOPHY OF UNIVERSAL ARCHITECTURE

The ideal of modern architecture being an articulated mechanical adequacy that not only frees human phenomena from robotism of inevitable survival functions; but also, and moreover, tends towards progressive material un-selfconsciousness of control, of such adequate mechanics of universal life intercourse, as to bring into high relief the residuary 'mental', or 'time', awareness of only the eternally ex-static: harmonic, phenomena – thus bespeaking, via the contemporarily, and embryonically, envisioned universal architecture (i.e., radionic-time-growth composition, progressively comple-mentary to, and synchronizable with, a comprehensive life concept, scienti-fically arrived at, and harmonically sustained), an eventual elimination of the 'time' phenomena (a 'past' and 'future' based on auto-suggestive procrastinating fallacial concept of the 'would-be static entrenchment of the selfish ego') which 'time' phenomena blinds the ego to the infinity of delight of the eternal 'now', visible only through the universally concerned intellectual optics of integrity.

Verbal Graph of Philosophy of Cosmic Trinity of Stability (no pure condition) (speaking in terms of direction not statics).

1. INDUSTRY=eternal life force – dynamics – time relative mobility within conscious limits of cosmic sphere between relatively smallest and largest mental radial activity

2. SCIENCE =radial direction life-in – philosophy
=functionalism, essential extraction, refines toward selective simplicity of the infinity of unity.

Dissection
singularity – male – compression –
pressure – internal – intellect –
abstraction – eternity – subconscious.

3. ART=radial direction of life-out – knowledge
=harmony – time synchronization – refines towards selective multiplicity of infinity of completeness.

Composition
plurality – female – tension –
vacuum – external – sense –
articulation – time – conscious

PHILOSOPHY OF 'GROWTH' (synchronizing design with scientific cosmology of relative radionic expanding spheres – entropy – cosmic radiation increase – life cell continuity)

The whole composition should never be dependent on the relative success of any one unit: and, or, positively stated, all units should be independently (flexibly, angularly) aligned to the whole composition of structure, and therefore progressively replaceable by ever more adequate unit solutions, thus making for an evolutionary growth to an intellectually (selectively) refining totality, within a time span, relatively exquisite, as compared to the gross tardiness of 'naturally' eliminating destructive staticism, which latter invokes revolutionary, and iconoclastic, replacements of 'whole old compositions', when the static ideology becomes dominantly incompetent, through a plurality of compromise paralysed cells.

We apparently may be directionary, that is radially, but not time specific, when in relatively radiant control of our being. Wherefor we should determine our 'ideal' and 'shoot' for it. Though our concept of an empirically derived material 'goal', by virtue of working of scientific postulate of positive growth, (Entropy, i.e., law of increase of the random element, cosmic radiation force increase, etc.) original 'goal', by time of accomplishment, so relatively 'small'

that highest urge of unselfish ambition, is niggardly in proportion to unforeseen, unexpected, unconscious attainments, en route our mirage-like, historically-articulated, ideal, when served with integrity.

TYPICAL LANGUAGE OF DESIGN OF ESSENTIAL PHILOSOPHY UNIVERSAL ARCHITECTURE

Angular modulus of unification.
Metrical measure for radial or time distances.
Flexible joints for force intercourse.
Unity of assembly contact = 'hook-up'.
Segregation of function with specific solution in terms of dynamics, with ultimate material choice on basis of specific economy, i.e., mean of longevity, transportability, availability, workability.
Centralization of mental activity – decentralization of physical activity (either personal or communal or industrial).
Maximum lightness – consistent economy.
Up and out (fountain like=deliquescence).
Use forces – do not fight them.
Material structure essentially functional – harmonies mobile and abstract from zero to selective sense limits.
Progress by creation – by increase in volume.
Complete independence of survival and sustenance bespeaking communities of choice not imposition.
No secrets.
High longevity through flexure and load flow in tension.
One for all and all for one.
Specific longevity consistent with economic adequacy and industrial continuity, citable each unit of composition.
Relatively immediate availability in time or space – mutability and mobility. Whole composition or unit thereof.
General dynamic awareness that all elements go through solid, liquid and gaseous state, with automatic, spheroidal, volume increase, plus impact load flow distributability, indicating that we should SOLVE:

1. Structurally-balanced tension functions by elements in solid fibre-pack state; and
2. Structurally-balanced compression functions by elements in spheroidal liquid state; and
3. Eccentric loads, impact to structure, etc., by initial exposure of solid, load-flowing, tension member; compassing load-flowing, liquid, compression member; which, in turn, compasses ultimate shock-absorption member, which is element in its elastic, gaseous state, as – for example – life cell, or football containing 90% water, 10% air.

Universal Architecture's Town Plan – Cosmos=World, and particularly dry land portion of World's surface, without national reference=54 acres per person in A.D.2000. (England and R.I. now average four persons per acre.) 26% Earth surface is dry land of which 50% 'Habitable' – whole human family two billion in A.D.2000 can stand on Island of Bermuda. Ample room. Town Plan based on primary World airways utilizing prevailing winds and great circle courses.

LIFE CONTINUITY VIA UNIVERSAL ARCHITECTURE

Consistent with foregoing concepts of universal architecture, and quite inconsistent traditional dogmatic orders, archi-tecture – Stone Age to International – (inclusive), following clippings from newspapers – front-paged in Chicago and back-paged in N.Y.C. (industrial geography phenomenon) are of extraordinary importance, and pertinence, to this article. Supplementing them by review of fact that biology indicates that, with internal and external mechanical aids, life cell group of tree structure in its geometrical progression of volume increase, in its continuity of angular cell pack outgrowth, may attain infinity: and reviewing fact that life cell of human is identical to that of tree, and has, if scientifically understood, more able mechanical supporting structure for survival: and reviewing recent professionally accepted knowledge of glandular phenomena, which indicates life cell grouping may replenish to infinity human structure and mechanics, via colloidal chemistry, by catalytic prevention glandular cell paralysis through cloture; the concluding paragraphs may not seem specious.

A back section Sunday *New York Times*, 24 January 1932. (Excerpt)
'Dr Robert A. Millikan revealed last night apparently decisive proof of his theory that cosmic rays signal the continuous rebirth instead of the destruction of the material universe. The consensus of opinion of one hundred scientists, including Dr Albert Einstein, who heard the talk at California Institute of Technology, was that Dr Millikan finally has refuted the theory of Sir James Jeans, who holds that the mysterious rays are "death wails" instead of "birth cries" of atoms.'

The front-page *Chicago Sunday Tribune*, 3 January 1932. (Excerpt)
'SCIENCE FINDS COSMIC CLEW TO HUMAN DESTINY. DR COMPTON EXPLAINS.'
'If we wish to retain any exact relation between cause and effect, we must postulate a world related to the physical world, but regarding which experiment gives us no information, in which the events may be determined.

'In such a non-physical world it is possible that motives and thoughts may play a determining part, while in the physical world in which such things remain unnoticed, events appear to follow the laws of chance.

'The new physics does not suggest a solution of the old question of how mind acts on matter. It does definitely, however, admit the possibility of such an action, and suggests where the action may take effect.'

A back-page *New York Times*, 2 February 1932.
'Dr Michael Pupin, who received a few days ago the John Fritz Gold Medal, the highest honor bestowed by the engineering profession in the United States, predicted yesterday that a complete transformation of civilization was coming as the result of our growing powers of electricity.' Dr Pupin said, 'Electricity is a celestial gift to man. It has the power to lift the life of man higher than any of us have yet dared to dream about. When man has achieved control of that power, the miracles of the present age will seem insignificant in comparison and man may at last achieve an existence akin to that of the Olympian Gods.' Dr Pupin asserted that while science is making rapid strides in conquering the material universe, man's spiritual progress has lagged. He spoke mournfully of the 'tragic lack of development of human love'. 'Hatreds, ignorance, petty jealousies, and prejudices are responsible for the wars, business depressions, and other sufferings of the world', adding that 'as long as man's spiritual being is retarded in its growth we will be unable to enjoy to the fullest the fruits of material progress.'

Architecture of past has not considered such 'news' as directly inclusive. Architecture of Universal now does consider such news as directly inclusive.

DREAM CASTLES

Galsworthy, in an essay entitled 'Castles in Spain', in the annual *Yale Review* for 1922, wrote that 'on 8 July 1401, the Dean and Chapter of Seville assembled in the Court of Elms and solemnly resolved "Let us build a church so great that those who come after us may think us mad to have attempted it", and it took five generations one hundred and fifty years to build it.' Galsworthy then went on to cite twentieth-century structures such as Woolworth building and Panama Canal, and to compare the fact that the Sevillians built entirely for their spiritual needs and thought naught of the practical needs of those who built; while the twentieth centurist apparently built entirely for his immediate needs without spiritual consideration, going on to suggest, however, that a middle course would develop – balancing life. The article, beautifully written, was an inspirational catalytic for the writer, to so extraordinary extent [*sic*], that he resolved that, no matter how mad it might seem, to set *his* ideal on a universal architecture so great that it might not only bring this result about, but also be the primary cause, and means of realization, of science's timidly voiced observation that continuity of life in its present structure, without the phenomena of total death and replacement, was theoretically discernible. It has always been the writer's notion that effective results may only be obtained through external articulation, for any brain-conceivable problem (that wishes are reasonable, as we can only wish within our thought limits, and all thoughts are in the terms of experience-compositions, in which dynamic principles are, often obscurely, embedded, but derivable through de-selfing thought). But as man first conceived of flying, he pictured himself sprouting, or grafting on wings, on personal equation basis.

He accomplished flying (overcoming gravity) by an external intellectual articulation, i.e. a machine, which need not physically encumber the human, when not flying – as would wings – so, while eternal life and 'fountains of youth' have been despaired of as personal adjustment developments, the new universal architecture of a physical – intellectual – scientific external machine holds promise of accomplishing the life balance.

Major attainment of this ecstatic life dream may take 150 light years, or 150 world years, we cannot be time specific, but these aware (as for instance, Mr Wells, in his current contributions) of the relative tempo-increase of physical articulation attainment, of the human phenomena (on a geometrical progression basis, in comparison to past rates of accomplishment, in proportion to world time cycles, as based on the rhythm of natural cycles of astronomical relationship), will have high faith of a reasonably immediate dawn of synchronization. Those who are scientifically minded know that the nature of a mathematical equation is such that a problem adequately stated is a problem solved. The writer can say no more in his personal equation language of 'Humpty-Dumpty', other than exhorting high countenance of the colloidal flux of science, industry, art, and life; to wit – have faith in the progressive intellectual revelations of the unity of truth, of the truth of unity, and of the unity and truth of the eternal now!

1933   CIAM:
Charter of Athens: tenets

CIAM II in Frankfurt in 1929, which was concerned with 'Minimum Living-Standard Housing', and CIAM III in Brussels in 1930 ('Rational Utilization of Building Sites'), confronted the delegates more and more urgently with problems of town planning. In order to carry the discussion further, the methods of presentation had to be unified. A preparatory committee (CIRPAC) met three times (Berlin 1931, Barcelona 1932, Paris 1933) before CIAM IV could take place in July and August 1933 on board the *Patris* between Marseilles and Athens. The results of these deliberations concerning 'The Functional City' were later set out by Le Corbusier in the *Charter of Athens* (1941), paragraphs 71–95 of which constitute essential tenets.

71. The majority of the cities studied today present a picture of chaos: these cities in no way fulfil their destiny, which is to satisfy the primordial biological and psychological needs of their inhabitants.

The cities analysed on the occasion of the Congress of Athens through the efforts of the national groups of the 'Congrès Internationaux d'Architecture Moderne' were thirty-three in number: Amsterdam, Athens, Brussels, Baltimore, Bandung, Budapest, Berlin, Barcelona, Charleroi, Cologne, Como, Dalat (Vietnam), Detroit, Dessau, Frankfurt, Geneva, Genoa, The Hague, Los Angeles, Littoria, London, Madrid, Oslo, Paris, Prague, Rome, Rotterdam, Stockholm, Utrecht, Verona, Warsaw, Zagreb, Zürich. They illustrate the history of the white race in the most varying climates and latitudes. All of them bear witness to the same phenomenon: the disorder introduced by the machine into a state of affairs which had previously been relatively harmonious, as well as the absence of any serious attempt at adaptation. In every one of these cities man is subjected to annoyance. Everything that surrounds him suffocates and crushes him. None of those things necessary for his physical and moral health has been preserved or introduced. A human crisis is raging in all the big cities and spreading its effects throughout the country. The city no longer serves its function, which is to shelter human beings and shelter them well'

72. This situation reveals the ceaseless increase of private interests since the beginning of the machine age.

The pre-eminence of private initiatives, inspired by personal interest and the lure of profit, is at the bottom of this regrettable state of affairs. Up to now, no authority, conscious of the nature and importance of the movement towards mechanization, has taken steps to avert the damage for which in practice no one can be held responsible. For a hundred years enterprises were left to chance. The building of housing and factories, construction of roads, waterways, and railways, everything multiplied in a haste and with an individual violence not preceded by thought or planning. Today the harm has been done. The cities are inhuman and the ferocity of a few private interests has given rise to the suffering of countless individuals.

73. The ruthless violence of private interests disastrously upsets the balance between the thrust of economic forces on the one hand and the weakness of administrative control and the powerlessness of social solidarity on the other.

The sense of administrative responsibility and of social solidarity are daily shattered by the vigorous and constantly renewed onslaught of private interest. These various sources of energy stand in perpetual opposition and when one attacks, the other defends itself. In this unfortunately unequal struggle, private interest most often triumphs, guaranteeing the success of the stronger at the expense of the weaker. But good sometimes springs from the very excess of evil, and the immense material and moral chaos of the modern city will perhaps bring into being city legislation which, supported by a strong sense of administrative responsibility, will introduce the regulations indispensable to human health and dignity.

74. Although cities are in a state of permanent transformation, their development takes place without either precision or control, and without any account being taken of the principles of contemporary town planning worked out by qualified specialist bodies.

The principles of modern town planning have been developed by the work of countless technicians: technicians in the art of building, technicians of health, technicians of social organization. These principles have been the subject of articles, books, congresses, public and private debates. But they still have to be acknowledged by the administrative authorities responsible for watching over the fate of cities, who are often hostile to the major transformations called for by these new insights. Authority must first be enlightened, then it must act. Clearsightedness and energy may succeed in bringing the dangerous situation under control.

75. On both the spiritual and material planes, the city must ensure individual liberty and the advantages of collective action.

Individual liberty and collective action are the two poles between which the game of life is played. Every enterprise aimed at improving the human lot must take account of these two factors. If it does not succeed in satisfying their frequently contradictory demands it is doomed to certain failure. It is in any case impossible to co-ordinate them harmoniously without working out in advance a carefully studied programme that leaves nothing to chance.

76. All dimensions within the city plan must be based exclusively on human proportions.

The natural measurements of man must serve as a basis for the scale of everything related to living and the various functions of existence: the scale of measurements applied to surfaces and distances, the scale of distances considered in relation to the natural walking pace of man, the scale of timetables which must be determined by reference to the daily course of the sun.

77. The keys to town planning are to be found in the four functions: housing, work, recreation (during leisure), and traffic.

Town planning expresses the way of life of an age. Up to now it has attacked only one problem, that of traffic. It has confined itself to cutting avenues or laying down streets, thereby forming islands of buildings whose utilization is left to haphazard private enterprise. This is a narrow and inadequate view of its task. Town planning has four principal functions, namely: first, to provide the inhabitants with salubrious housing, that is to say, places in which space, fresh air, and sunshine are plentifully guaranteed; second, to organize workplaces so that, instead of being a painful thraldom, work will regain its character as a natural human activity; third, to set up the installations necessary for the good use of leisure, rendering it beneficial and productive; fourth, to establish links between these various organizations by means of a traffic network that facilitates movement from place to place while respecting the rights of all. These four functions, which are the four keys of town planning, cover an immense field, since town planning is the outcome of a way of thinking applied to public life by means of a technique of action.

78. Planning will determine the structure of each of the sectors assigned to the four key functions and will fix their respective locations within the whole.

Since the Congress of Athens, the four key functions of town planning demand special arrangements offering each of them the most favourable conditions for the development of its particular activity, in order that they may be manifested in all their fullness and bring order and classification into the usual conditions of life, work and culture. Town planning, by taking account of this need, will transform the face of cities, will break with the crushing constraint of practices that have lost their raison d'être and will open an inexhaustible field of action to creators. Each key function will have its own autonomy based on the circumstances arising out of climate, topography and customs; they will be considered as entities to which will be assigned territories and locations, for whose equipment and installation all the prodigious resources of modern technology will be mobilized. In this distribution, consideration will be given to the vital needs of the individual, not the interest or profit of any particular group. Town planning must guarantee individual liberty at the same time as it takes advantage of the benefits of collective action.

79. The cycle of daily living – housing, work, recreation (recuperation) – will be regulated by town planning with a strict insistence on time saving, the dwelling being regarded as the very centre of town planning concerns and the focal point of all measures.

The desire to reintroduce 'natural conditions' into daily life would seem at first sight to call for a greater horizontal extension of cities; but the need to regulate the various activities by the duration of the sun's course is opposed to this idea, the disadvantage of which is that it imposes distances out of proportion to the available time. The dwelling place is the centre of the town planner's concern and relative distances will be governed by its position in the town plan in conformity with the solar day of twenty-four hours, which determines the rhythm of men's activity and gives the correct measure to all their undertakings.

80. The new mechanical speeds have disrupted the urban environment, creating permanent danger, causing traffic jams and paralysing communications, and interfering with hygiene.

Mechanical vehicles ought to be agents of liberation and, through their speed, to bring about a valuable gaining of time. But their accumulation and their concentration at certain points have become both an obstacle to movement and the source of constant danger. Moreover, they have introduced into urban life numerous factors injurious to health. Their combustion gases spread in the air are harmful to the lungs and their noise induces in man a condition of permanent nervous irritability. The speeds that are now available arouse the temptation to daily escape, far away, into nature, spread the taste for a mobility without restraint or measure and favour ways of life which, by breaking up the family, profoundly disturb the foundations of society. They condemn men to spend exhausting hours in all sorts of vehicles and little by little to lose the exercise of the healthiest and most natural of all functions: walking.

81. The principle of urban and suburban traffic must be revised. A classification of available speeds must be drawn up. The reform of zoning that brings the key functions of the city into harmony will create between them natural links, which in turn will be reinforced by the establishment of a rational network of major thoroughfares.

Zoning that takes account of the key functions – housing, work, recreation – will bring order to the urban territory. Traffic, the fourth function, must have only one aim: to bring the other three usefully into communication. Great transformations are inevitable. The city and its region must be equipped with a network of roads exactly proportionate to the uses and purposes, and in conformity with the modern technology of transport. The means of travel must be classified and differentiated and for each of them a way must be created appropriate to the exact nature of the vehicles employed. Traffic thus regulated becomes a steady function that in no way interferes with the structure of housing or of workplaces.

82. Town planning is a three-dimensional science, not a two-dimensional one. By introducing the element of height it will become possible to solve the problems of modern traffic and of leisure, through utilizing the free spaces thus created.

The key functions, housing, work and recreation develop inside built volumes subject to three imperious necessities: sufficient space, sun, ventilation. These volumes depend not only on the soil and its two dimensions, but above all on a third: height. It is by making use of height that town planning will recover the free areas of land necessary to communications and the spaces to be used for leisure. A distinction must be made between sedentary functions, which take place inside volumes in which the third dimension plays the most important part, and functions of transport, which use only two dimensions, are linked to the soil and for which height plays a role only rarely and on a small scale, as, for example, when changes of level are introduced to cope with certain intense concentrations of vehicles.

83. The city must be studied within the totality of its region of influence. A regional plan will replace the simple municipal plan. The limit of the agglomeration will coincide with the radius of its economic action.

The data of a town planning problem are given by the totality of the activities carried on not only in the town, but in the whole region of which it is the centre. The town's raison d'être must be sought and expressed in figures that will allow prediction of the stages of a plausible future development. The same work applied to the secondary agglomerations will provide a reading of the general situation. Allocations, restrictions, compensations can be decided that will assign to each town surrounded by its region its own particular character and destiny. Thus each one will take its place and its rank in the general economy of the country. The result will be a clear demarcation of the limits of the region. This is total town planning, capable of bringing balance to both the province and the country.

84. The city, henceforth defined as a functional unit, must grow harmoniously in each of its parts, having at its disposal spaces and links within which, in a balanced way, the stages of its development may be inscribed.

The city will assume the character of an enterprise studied in advance and subjected to the rigour of an overall plan. Wise foresight will have sketched its future, described its nature, anticipated the scope of its developments and limited their excess in advance. Subordinated to the needs of the region, destined to incorporate the four key functions, the city will no longer be the chaotic result of random enterprises. Its development, instead of producing a disaster, will be a crowning achievement. And the growth of its population will not lead to that inhuman crush which is one of the plagues of big cities.

85. It is urgently necessary for every city to establish its programme and promulgate laws that will enable this to be put into effect.

Chance will be replaced by foresight, programme will succeed improvisation. Each case will be integrated into the regional plan; the land will be measured and assigned to various activities: there will be clear regulations governing the project which will be started immediately and carried out bit by bit by successive stages. The Law will establish permanent building regulations providing each key function with the means to achieve optimum expression, through being situated in the most favourable locations and at the most useful distances. The Law must also allow for the protection and care of areas that will one day be occupied. It will have the right to authorize – or to forbid; it will foster all well-conceived initiatives but will take care that they fit into the overall plan and are always subordinate to the collective interests that constitute the public good.

86. The programme must be based upon analyses rigorously carried out by specialists. It must foresee the stages of progress in time and in space. It must gather into a fruitful harmony the natural resources of the site, the topography of the whole area, the economic facts, the sociological needs and the spiritual values.

The work will no longer be limited to the precarious plan of the geometer who, governed by the chance location of the suburbs, designs the solid lumps of tenements and the scattered dust of building developments. It will be a true biological creation made up of clearly defined organs capable of fulfilling to perfection their essential functions. The resources of the soil will be analyzed and the restraints which they impose recognized; the general ambience will be studied and a hierarchy of the natural values established. The main thoroughfares will be decided upon and located in the right positions and the nature of their equipment determined according to the use for which they are intended. A growth curve will express the economic future envisaged for the town. Infrangible laws will guarantee the inhabitants comfortable housing, good working conditions and the enjoyment of leisure. The soul of the city will be brought to life by the lucidity of the plan.

87. For the architect concerned with the tasks of town planning all measurements must be based on the human scale.

Architecture, after its gross distortions during the last hundred years, must once more be placed at the service of man. It must abandon sterile pomp, must care for the individual and create for his happiness the installations that make up his environment so as to facilitate all his actions. Who could carry out the measures necessary for the successful accomplishment of this task if not the architect, who possesses a perfect knowledge of man, who has abandoned designs based on illusory aesthetic considerations, and who, by precisely adapting means to the desired ends, will create an order that bears within it its own poetry?

88. The initial nucleus of town planning is a housing cell (a dwelling) and its insertion in a group forming a housing unit of efficient size.

If the cell is the primordial biological element, the home, that is to say the shelter of a family, constitutes the social cell. The building of this home, after more than a century of subjection to the brutal games of speculation, must become a humane undertaking. The home is the initial nucleus of town planning. It protects man's growth, shelters the joys and sorrows of his daily life. If it has to have sunshine and fresh air inside, it also has to be extended outside by various communal installations. To make it easier to supply the dwelling with communal services that will facilitate the provision of food, education, medical assistance, and leisure enjoyments, it will be necessary to group them in 'housing units' of an efficient size.

89. Interrelationships within the urban space between dwellings, workplaces and the facilities devoted to leisure will be established with this housing unit as the starting point.

The first of the functions to which the town planner has to give his attention is housing – and good housing. People also have to work, and to do so under conditions that demand a serious revision of the practices at present in operation. Offices, workshops and factories must be fitted out in such a way as to ensure the wellbeing necessary to the accomplishment of this second function. Finally, the third function must not be neglected: recreation, the cultivation of body and mind. The town planner must provide the necessary sites and premises.

90. To fulfil this great task it is essential to utilize the resources of modern technology. The latter, through the collaboration of its specialists, will support the art of building with all the security of science and enrich it with the inventions and resources of the age.

The machine age has introduced new techniques which are one of the causes of the disorder and confusion of cities. Nevertheless it is from them that we must demand the solution of the problem. Modern building techniques have established new methods, provided new facilities, permitted new dimensions. They have opened an entirely new cycle in the history of architecture. The new buildings will be not merely of a size, but also of a complexity unknown till now. In order to accomplish the multiple task imposed upon him, the architect, at all stages of the enterprise, must call upon the aid of numerous specialists.

91. The course of events will be fundamentally influenced by political, social and economic factors . . .

It is not enough to admit the necessity for a 'land law' and certain principles of construction. To pass from theory to action requires the conjunction of the following factors: a political power of the kind we want – clearsighted, with firm convictions and determined to bring into being the best living conditions that have been worked out and committed to paper; an enlightened population that will understand, desire, and demand what the specialists have envisaged for it; an economic situation that makes it possible to embark upon and to pursue building projects which in some cases will be considerable. It is possible, however, that even at a period when things are at a very low ebb, when political, moral, and economic conditions are extremely unfavourable, the need to build decent housing will suddenly appear an imperious obligation and that this obligation will give to politics, social life, and the economy precisely the coherent aim and programme which they lacked.

92. And here architecture will not be the least of the forces at work.

Architecture presides over the destiny of the city. It orders the structure of the home, that essential cell of the urban tissue, whose health, gaiety, and harmony are subject to its decisions. It groups homes in dwelling units whose success will depend upon the accuracy of its calculations. It reserves in advance the free spaces in the midst of which will rise volumes built in harmonious proportions. It organizes the extensions of the home, the places of work, the areas devoted to relaxation. It establishes the traffic network that brings the various zones into contact. Architecture is responsible for the well-being and beauty of the city. It is architecture that sees to its creation and improvement, and it is architecture's task to choose and distribute the various elements whose felicitous proportions will constitute a harmonious and lasting work. Architecture holds the key to everything.

93. The scale of work to be undertaken as a matter of urgency for the reorganization of cities on the one hand, and on the other the infinitely fragmented state of land ownership, are two opposing realities.

Works of major importance must be undertaken without delay, since every town in the world, ancient or modern, reveals the same defects arising from the same causes. But no partial solution should be embarked upon that does not fit into the framework of the town and of the region as they have been laid down by a wide-ranging study and a broad overall plan. This plan will necessarily contain parts that can be put into effect immediately and others that will have to be postponed to indefinite dates. Numerous pieces of property will have to be expropriated and will become the subject of negotiation. It is at this point that we have reason to fear the sordid game of speculation which so often crushes in the cradle great enterprises animated by concern for the public good. The problem of land ownership and possible land requisition arises in towns, on their periphery and extends throughout the zone, however large or small, that makes up their region.

94. The dangerous contradiction noted here poses one of the most hazardous questions of the age: the urgent need to regulate, by legal means, the distribution of all usable ground, in order to bring the vital needs of the individual into complete harmony with collective needs.

For years major building projects, all over the world, have come to grief on the petrified laws governing private property. The soil – the territory of the country – ought to be available at any moment and at its fair value, estimated before plans have been drawn up. The ground should be open to mobilization when it is a matter of the general interest. All kinds of unpleasantness have come upon the people who were unable to measure accurately the extent of technological transformations and their repercussions on public and private life. Lack of town planning is the cause of the anarchy that reigns in the organization of cities and the equipment of industries. Because people have failed to understand the rules, the countryside has been emptied, towns have been filled beyond all reason, concentrations of industry have taken place haphazardly, workers' dwellings have become hovels. Nothing was done to safeguard man. The result is catastrophic and it is almost identical in every country. It is the bitter fruit of a hundred years of the undirected development of the machine.

95. Private interest will be subordinated to the collective interest.

Left to himself, man is quickly crushed by difficulties of all sorts which he has to surmount. On the other hand, if he is subjected to too many collective constraints his personality becomes stifled. Individual rights have nothing to do with vulgar private interest. The latter, which heaps wealth upon a minority while condemning the rest of the social mass to a mediocre life, merits severe restriction. It must everywhere be subordinated to the collective interest, every individual having access to the basic joys: the wellbeing of the home, the beauty of the city.

1943 Walter Gropius/Martin Wagner: A programme for city reconstruction

In 1937 CIAM V met in Paris ('Housing and Leisure'), in 1947 CIAM VI met in Bridgwater ('Confirmation of the Aims of CIAM'). The Germans who took part in these congresses were emigrés. For with the internal political developments of 1933 the development of the new architecture was brought to a sudden end. The Bauhaus in Berlin was closed for good; all the personalities of the new architecture were removed from administrative and teaching posts or forbidden to work any more. Breuer, Gropius, Hilberseimer, May, Mendelsohn, Meyer, Mies, and Wagner – to name only these – immediately or later left the country. With their arrival America gained the leading role in the world of the new architecture.

1. Lot and block rehabilitation has not been successful. Sweeping 'square mile' rehabilitation has become a necessity since we have recognized the interrelationship of the town with its region.

2. Former suggestions such as 'The City Beautiful' and other pictorial schemes have proved to be incomplete. First, action should be started by preparing legal, financial and administrative instruments to enable the planners to conceive and work out reliable master plans.

3. Places of work and their relation to places of living should form the pivot of all reconstruction work.

4. First of all the existing cities should be relieved of congestion and high blood pressure by removing those who cannot be permanently employed. Resettled around small industries in new 'townships' these people would regain their productive capacity and purchasing power.

5. The new townships should settle along super-highways and be connected by fast feeder roads with the old city centre.

6. The size of the townships should be limited by the pedestrian range to keep them within a human scale.

7. The 'townships' must be surrounded by their own farm belts.

8. Speculation often promotes blight and obsolescence. Therefore the community should own the land. The dwelling lots should be rented, though the houses may be owned.

9. The administrative setup of a township should take the form of a self-contained unit with its independent local government. This will strengthen community spirit.

10. From five to ten – or more – neighbourhood townships may be combined into a 'countyship' with an administration governing activities beyond the reach of a single unit. Its size and administrative setup should also serve as a model for the basic neighbourhood units of the old towns to be reconstructed.

11. It is suggested that the size of a township remain stable. Flexibility within its boundaries must therefore be achieved by making the housing facilities elastic.

12. Parallel to the resettlement of idle labour in new townships, a second process must take place; acquisition of land by the community of the old city. For not until that process of pooling land has been completed can the next step – the redistribution of land – be taken, for the final reconstruction of the city.

1947　A post-war appeal: fundamental demands

Germany 1945: countryside and cities have been laid waste; the centres from which the new architecture once radiated an influence on the world are fields of rubble; the physical and psychological collapse is unparalleled. Those who had been scattered gather together only slowly. The years of want suffocate the first courageous endeavours: the devastation of life exceeds the strength they were able to preserve during the dark years of dictatorship. Before resignation spreads, Alphons Leitl manages to resuscitate architectural discussion. The first numbers of his periodical *Baukunst und Werkform* are at once a stocktaking and a forum for ideas. In 1947 it carried an appeal that has long since been forgotten.

The collapse has destroyed the visible world that constituted our life and our work. When it took place we believed, with a sense of liberation, that now we should be able to return to work. Today, two years later, we realize how much the visible breakdown is merely the expression of a spiritual devastation and we are tempted to sink into despair. We have been reduced to fundamentals and the task must be tackled afresh from this point.

All the peoples of the earth are faced with this task; for our people it is a case of to be or not to be. Upon the conscience of us, the creative, lies the obligation to build the new visible world that makes up our life and our work. Conscious of this responsibility we demand:

1. When they are rebuilt, the big cities must be divided up into a new association of viable local sections, each of which is a self-contained unit; the old city centre must acquire new life as the cultural and political core.

2. The heritage that has been destroyed must not be reconstructed historically; in order to fulfil new tasks it must be rebuilt in a new form.

3. In our country towns – the last visible symbols of German history – a living unity must be achieved between the old buildings and streets and modern residential and industrial edifices.

4. Complete reorganization also demands planned reconstruction of the German village.

5. For dwelling houses and for our public buildings, for furniture and fittings, we call for the replacement of over-specialized or wretchedly utilitarian shapes by simple and valid designs.

For only the validly simple can be used on a multiple scale. Architecture can succeed only on the basis of a concentration of effort, of communal endeavour in design office and workshop.

In a spirit of self-sacrifice we call upon all men of good will.

The appeal on page 148 is signed by

Otto Bartning | Willi Baumeister | Eugen Blanck | Walter Dierks |
Richard Döcker | Egon Eiermann | Karl Foerster | Richard Hamann |
Gustav Hassenpflug | Otto Haupt | Werner Hebebrand | Carl Georg Heise |
Carl Oskar Jatho | Hans Leistikow | Alphons Leitl | Georg Leowald |
Rudolf Lodders | Alfred Mahlau | Gerhard Marcks | Ewald Mataré |
Ludwig Neundörfer | Walter Passarge | Max Pechstein | Lilly Reich |
Paul Renner | Wilhelm Riphahn | Hans Schmidt | Lambert Schneider |
Fritz Schumacher | Rudolf Schwarz | Otto Ernst Schweizer |
Hans Schwippert | Max Taut | Heinrich Tessenow | Otto Völckers |
Robert Vorhoelzer | Wilhelm Wagenfeld | Hans Warnecke

1947   Frederick Kiesler:
Magical Architecture

During the war French Surrealist circles were centres of resistance to the spirit-killing influence of the dictatorship. When the friends emerged from their hiding places or returned from emigration, their attitude was unbroken. In 1947 they organized an International Post-war Exhibition of Surrealism. Frederick Kiesler, who in 1926 was demanding 'Vital Architecture' and the 'Space City,' collaborated with Max Ernst, Miró, Matta, Duchamp, and others to produce in the 'Hall of Superstition' a room in which architecture, sculpture, and painting shared equally as a continuum of the arts. The idea of the collective work, advocated by the De Stijl group, came to life again – though in an entirely different form.

The nineteenth century saw the twilight and the first quarter of the twentieth century saw the dissolution of the unity Architecture-Painting-Sculpture. The Renaissance throve on this unity. The people's faith in the happiness of the beyond carried it on its wings.

Our new period (1947) has rediscovered the social conscience. The instinctive need for a new unity has been reborn. The hope of this unity is no longer situated in the beyond, but in the HERE AND NOW.

The new reality of the plastic arts is manifested as a correlation of facts not based solely on the perceptions of the five senses, but also answering the need of the psyche.

'Modern functionalism' in architecture is dead. In so far as the 'function' was a survival – without even an examination of the Kingdom of the Body upon which it rested – it came to grief and was exhausted in the mystique hygiene+ aestheticism. (The Bauhaus, Le Corbusier's system, etc.)

The Hall of Superstitions presents a first effort towards a continuity Architecture–Painting–Sculpture, using the means of expression of our epoch. The problem is a double one: (1) to create a unity; (2) of which the constituents Painting–Sculpture–Architecture will be transmuted one into the other.

I designed the spatial configuration. I invited the painters Duchamp, Max Ernst, Matta, Miró, Tanguy and the sculptors Hare and Maria to carry out my plan. They collaborated with fervour. I conceived each part of the whole, form and content, specially for each artist. There were no misunderstandings.
If the totality did not work it would be entirely my fault, because they adhered strictly to my plan of correlation.
This collective work, created not by artists of one single profession, but by the block Architect–Painter–Sculptor, plus the Poet (the author of the theme),

even in the event of failure, represents the most stimulating promise of development for our plastic arts.

I oppose to the mysticism of Hygiene, which is the superstition of 'Functional Architecture', the realities of a Magical Architecture rooted in the totality of the human being, and not in the blessed or accursed parts of this being.

1949 Henry van de Velde:
Forms (excerpt)

Henry van de Velde, who proposed Gropius as his successor in Weimar after the First World War, returned to Belgium in 1925 and in 1947 settled at Oberägeri on the Zuger See. From there, as though from a look-out post, he followed the work of his friends and former comrades in arms. He apportioned praise and blame and became an authority whose approval could be relied upon for anyone who boldly pursued the path laid down by van de Velde in his pre-war programmatic writings. On rare occasions van de Velde, in addition to his memoirs, still wrote magazine articles lauding the beauty of purely functional forms.

Purely functional forms. They are *all* members of one *family*, whatever their specific function and purpose. They can all be traced to one and the same origin leading back through the centuries to the point when the cave man became aware of his most primitive needs (food, clothing, shelter) and of the means by which he could satisfy them.

Forms. These forms were born as though by magic! The spontaneous objectification of an idea springing from the dark, but wonderfully persistent, consciousness of the cave dweller.

From the stubborn perseverance of these primitive people there arose weapons, tools, domestic and agricultural appliances; the natural shelter was followed by the constructed dwelling.

Thus unfolds the wealth of forms *determined by their function.* They are all of the same kind, marked by the generating operation of intelligence, all equally pure, yes, equally perfect.

From its first beginnings in the Stone Age this formal language, in the course of centuries, took possession of all domains of the human mind. It followed the expanding needs and the evolution of civilization. The determining power of reason and the strict discipline imposed by intelligent insight remain guarantees of its innate purity, of the preservation of its essential qualities. But form is threatened by the terrifying advance of *fantasy*, by its seductions and befoulments. And yet the period of decadence, released by the assault of morbid growths and criminal attacks upon form, which can be traced from the beginning of the baroque into the nineteenth century, did not cause the source to dry up completely. Thus architects and decorators found themselves dethroned as soon as new and imperative needs called upon the inventive mind to create new forms. The engineer and the machine-builder reached back to the original tradition created by intelligent human insight, and their pure forms coincided with those that an *avant-garde* of pioneers of a 'new style' were seeking to bring into being as a result of reflecting upon the eternal, fundamental laws of reason (furniture, dwellings, public buildings).

It was at the beginning of the twentieth century that these new testimonies to purity of form made their appearance. When I declared that every form conceived by reason and exclusively determined by its function is pure and thus fulfils one condition, *sine qua non* of beauty, my less scrupulous opponents distorted this statement as meaning that if form corresponds to function, to the use which an object serves, it is necessarily beautiful . . .

In reality, the irrefutable products of the generative intelligence were merely *initial data*. From this moment, the possibility for purity to pour into the world existed; perhaps our era is waiting for a civilization that will once more elevate the morality of its contemporaries and restore to them the true concept of virtue. The new style will be characterized by dignity, refinement, nobility of outlook, and its dominion will bring us the awakening of good taste and the return to that beauty to which the heroes of the first crusade dedicated themselves: Ruskin with his gripping, eloquent professions of faith, William Morris with his noble art of disputation and his genius as a craftsman . . .

Stirred by the works of Gothic architecture, which surpassed all that had gone before and created a new equilibrium of unparalleled audacity, human sensibility experienced a hitherto unknown increase of enjoyment, of the ability to participate in the play of creative forces, a sensation imparted neither by the subtle but measured statics of Greek architecture nor by the restraint of Byzantine and Romanesque churches.

One primal ancestor, a giant. Like *Moses* descending from Sinai bearing the tables of the Law in his hand. Only now the laws of reason and of rational beauty are inscribed upon these tables.

One single source, creative reason. It produces the gold: pure forms. In combination with *perfection* (perfection of execution and the quality of the material) and ennobled by it, pure form rises on the steps of that altar where, achieving its loftiest manifestation, it is wedded to *beauty*.

But it is not every flower whose pistil is touched by the pollen shaken out by the trees in the garden of the ideal into which we have ventured; pure form too must advance beyond its starting point.

The lofty qualities which it owes to its purity will not perish in the process. The intervention of a magician, who prefers some of these 'pure forms' to others, rouses them from their slumber and interfuses with the purpose, which the malleable form fulfils only mechanically, the glow that represents the part he himself has played in their creation.

1950   Ludwig Mies van der Rohe:
Technology and architecture

In 1932 Mies moved to Berlin with the teachers and students of the Bauhaus and there continued it as a private institute. In July 1933 it was closed by the Gestapo. In summer 1937 Mies went to the USA; in 1938 he received an invitation to the Illinois Institute of Technology (IIT) in Chicago and a little later was commissioned to redesign the university campus. The first buildings went up in the years 1942–3. They introduced the second great phase of his architecture. In 1950 Mies delivered to the IIT the speech reproduced here.

Technology is rooted in the past. It dominates the present and tends into the future. It is a real historical movement – one of the great movements which shape and represent their epoch. It can be compared only with the Classic discovery of man as a person, the Roman will to power, and the religious movement of the Middle Ages. Technology is far more than a method, it is a world in itself. As a method it is superior in almost every respect. But only where it is left to itself, as in gigantic structures of engineering, there technology reveals its true nature. There it is evident that it is not only a useful means, but that it is something, something in itself, something that has a meaning and a powerful form – so powerful in fact, that it is not easy to name it. Is that still technology or is it architecture? And that may be the reason why some people are convinced that architecture will be outmoded and replaced by technology. Such a conviction is not based on clear thinking. The opposite happens. Wherever technology reaches its real fulfilment, it transcends into architecture. It is true that architecture depends on facts, but its real field of activity is in the realm of significance. I hope you will understand that architecture has nothing to do with the inventions of forms. It is not a playground for children, young or old. Architecture is the real battleground of the spirit. Architecture wrote the history of the epochs and gave them their names. Architecture depends on its time. It is the crystallization of its inner structure, the slow unfolding of its form. That is the reason why technology and architecture are so closely related. Our real hope is that they will grow together, that some day the one will be the expression of the other. Only then will we have an architecture worthy of its name: architecture as a true symbol of our time.

1954 Jacques Fillon: New games!

After the war the Charter of Athens became the essential basis for town planning throughout the world. It is at once textbook and dogma. As early as the beginning of the fifties, however, the first protests were already being raised against 'the functional city'. Significantly, they came from artists and men of letters who foresaw an immense loss of 'urban' life as the result of the disentanglement of living, working, recreation, and transportation.

Big cities are favourable to the pastime which we call *dérive*. *Dérive* is the technique of locomotion without a goal. It depends upon the influence of the external environment.

All houses are beautiful.

Architecture must reach the point of exciting passion. We could not consider any more limited constructional undertaking.

The new town planning is inseparable from the fortunately inescapable economic and social upheavals. We may assume that the revolutionary demands of an epoch are a function of the idea which this epoch has of happiness and wellbeing. The evaluation of leisure is something entirely serious.

We will issue a reminder that the task is to invent new games.

1957   Konrad Wachsmann:
Seven theses

When Konrad Wachsmann (b.1901 in Frankfurt/Oder, lives in Los Angeles) returned to Germany in 1954 for the first time since his emigration in 1933, he was both an astonished and an astonishing individualist. He was astonished to find that in the *Technischen Hochschulen* virtually no attention was paid to the standards required for the mass production of industrially manufactured building parts. Wachsmann was astonishing because in a short time he was able, with his methods and constructions, to arouse unrest among students preoccupied with technical conventions. Will the 'machine-builder' replace the architect? Wachsmann's theses amount to a starting-point for industrialized building.

Science and technology make possible the establishment of tasks whose solution demands precise study before end results can be formulated.

The machine is the tool of our age. It is the cause of those effects through which the social order manifests itself.

New materials, methods, processes, knowledge in the fields of statics and dynamics, planning techniques and sociological conditions must be accepted.

The building must evolve indirectly, obeying the conditions of industrialization, through the multiplication of cells and elements.

Modular systems of co-ordination, scientific experimental methods, the laws of automation, and precision influence creative thought.

Very complex static and mechanical problems demand the closest possible co-operation with industry and specialists in ideal teams composed of masters.

Human and aesthetic ideas will receive new impulses through the uncompromising application of contemporary knowledge and ability.

1958 Hundertwasser: Mould Manifesto against rationalism in architecture

On 4 July 1958 the Viennese painter Hundertwasser (b. 1928 in Vienna) read his *Verschimmelungs-Manifest* (Mould Manifest) in the abbey of Seckau. He had already protested a year earlier in an exhibition pamphlet against the '90-degree angles of Vienna'. 'In 1920 the pavement and the walls of the houses had to be constructed smooth, but in 1957 this is an insanity I cannot understand. The air raids of 1943 were a perfect automatic lesson in form; straight lines and their vacuous structures ought to have been blown to pieces, and so they were. Following this a transautomatism ought normally to have occurred ... But we are building cubes, cubes! Where is our conscience?'

Painting and sculpture are now free, for today anyone can produce any kind of work and afterwards exhibit it. In architecture, however, this fundamental freedom, which must be regarded as the precondition for any art, still does not exist, because in order to build one first has to have a diploma. Why?

Everyone should be able to build, and so long as this freedom to build does not exist, the planned architecture of today cannot be considered an art at all. Architecture with us is subject to the same censorship as painting in the Soviet Union. What are put into execution are merely wretched compromises standing in isolation and created by people with a bad conscience whose minds are dominated by the foot-rule!

No inhibitions should be placed upon the individual's desire to build! Everyone ought to be able and compelled to build, so that he bears real responsibility for the four walls within which he lives. We must face the risk that a crazy structure of this kind may later collapse, and we should not and must not shrink from the loss of life which this new way of building will, or at least may, exact. A stop must finally be put to the situation in which people move into their living quarters like hens and rabbits into their coops.

If one of these ramshackle structures built by its occupants is going to collapse, it generally starts cracking first so that they can run away. Thereafter the tenant will be more critical and creative in his attitude towards the dwellings he occupies and will strengthen the walls with his own hands if they seem to him too fragile.

+The material uninhabitability of the slums is preferable to the moral un-inhabitability of functional, utilitarian architecture. In the so-called slums only man's body can perish, but in the architecture ostensibly planned for man his soul perishes. Hence the principle of the slums, i.e. wildly proliferating architecture, must be improved and taken as our point of departure, not functional architecture.+

The passages marked with a + were added to the Mould Manifesto after the lecture at the Seckau congress.

Functional architecture has proved to be a wrong road, just like painting with a ruler. With giant strides we are approaching impractical, unusable, and finally uninhabitable architecture.

The great turning point – for painting, absolute tachist automatism – is for architecture absolute uninhabitability, which still lies ahead of us, because architecture limps thirty years behind.

Just as today, having gone beyond total tachist automatism, we are experiencing the miracle of transautomatism, so it is only after having overcome total uninhabitability and creative mouldering that we shall experience the miracle of a new, true, and free architecture. Since, however, we have not yet left total uninhabitability behind us, since we are unfortunately not yet in the midst of the transautomatism of architecture, we must first strive as rapidly as possible for total uninhabitability and creative mouldering in architecture.

A man in an apartment house must have the possibility of leaning out of his window and scraping off the masonry for as far as his hands reach. And he must be allowed to paint everything around pink as far as he can reach with a long brush, so that people can see from far away, from the street: a man lives there who differs from his neighbours, the little people who accept what is given to them! And he must be able to saw up the walls and carry out all sorts of alterations, even if the architectonically harmonious picture of a so-called masterpiece of architecture is thereby destroyed, and he must be able to fill his room with mud or plasticine.

But this is forbidden in the tenancy agreement!

It is time people themselves rebelled against being confined in box-constructions, in the same way as hens and rabbits are confined in cage-constructions that are equally foreign to their nature.

+ A cage-construction or utilitarian construction is a building that remains alien to all three categories of people that have to do with it!

1. The architect has no relationship to the building.
Even if he is the greatest architectural genius he cannot foresee what kind of person is going to live in it. The so-called human measurement in architecture is a criminal deception. Particularly when this measurement has emerged as an average value from a public opinion poll. +

2. The bricklayer has no relationship to the building.
If, for example, he wants to build a wall just a little differently in accordance with his personal ideas, if he has any, he loses his job. And anyhow he really doesn't care, because he isn't going to live in the building. +

3. The occupant has no relationship to the building.
Because he hasn't built it but has merely moved in. His human needs, his human space are certain to be quite different. And this remains a fact even if the architect and bricklayer try to build exactly according to the instructions of the occupant and employer. +

+ Only when architect, bricklayer and occupant are a unity, i.e. one and the same person, can one speak of architecture. Everything else is not architecture but the physical incarnation of a criminal act.

Architect-bricklayer-occupant are a trinity just like God the Father, Son and Holy Ghost. Note the similarity, almost the identity of the trinities. If the unity architect-bricklayer-occupant is lost there is no architecture, just as the objects being fabricated today cannot be regarded as architecture. Man must regain his critical-creative function, which he has lost and without which he ceases to exist as a human being. +

+ Criminal too is the use in architecture of the ruler, which, as may easily be proved, is to be considered an instrument that leads to the disintegration of the architectonic trinity. +

Merely to carry a straight line about with one ought to be, at least morally, forbidden. The ruler is the symbol of the new illiteracy. The ruler is the symptom of the new sickness of decadence.

We live today in a chaos of straight lines, in a jungle of straight lines. Anyone who doesn't believe this should take the trouble to count the straight lines all around him and he will understand; for he will never finish counting.

I have counted straight lines on a razor blade. Adding the linear and imaginary connexion with a second razor blade of the same make, which undoubtedly looks absolutely identical, this makes 1090 straight lines, and if we then add the packaging it yields 3000 straight lines per razor blade.

Not so very long ago the possession of straight lines was a privilege of kings, landowners, and the clever. Today every fool has millions of straight lines in his trouser pocket.

This jungle of straight lines, which increasingly hems us in like prisoners in a gaol, must be uprooted.

Until now man has always uprooted the jungle in which he found himself and set himself free. But first he has to become aware that he is living in a jungle, for this jungle has grown up surreptitiously, unnoticed by the population. And this time it is a jungle of straight lines.

Every modern architect in whose work the ruler or the compasses have played any part even for a second – and even if only in thought – must be rejected. Not to speak of the designing, drawing board, and modelmaking work, which has become not merely morbidly sterile but truly senseless. The straight line is ungodly and immoral. The straight line is not a creative, but a reproductive line. In it dwells not so much God and the human spirit as rather the comfort-loving, brainless mass ant.

Thus structures made up of straight lines, no matter how they crook, bend, overhang and actually perforate are untenable. They are the products of attachment born of fear: constructive architects are afraid to turn before it is too late to tachism, i.e. to uninhabitability.

When rust settles on a razor blade, when mould forms on a wall, when moss grows in the corner of a room and rounds off the geometrical angles, we ought to be pleased that with the microbes and fungi life is moving into the house, and more consciously than ever before we become witnesses of architectonic changes from which we have a great deal to learn.

The constructive functional architects' irresponsible mania for destruction is well known. They wanted simply to pull down the beautiful stucco-fronted houses of the nineties and *Art Nouveau* and put their own vacuous buildings in their place. I will cite Le Corbusier, who wanted to raze Paris to the ground and replace it with rectilinear monster constructions. To be fair, we ought now to pull down the buildings of Mies van der Rohe, Neutra, the Bauhaus, Gropius, Johnson, Le Corbusier, and so on, since in one generation they have become outmoded and morally unendurable.

The transautomatists and all those who have passed beyond uninhabitable architecture treat their predecessors more humanely, however. They no longer want to destroy.

In order to save functional architecture from moral ruin, a disintegrating preparation should be poured on the clean glass walls and smooth concrete surfaces, so that mould can settle on them.

+ It is time industry recognized its fundamental mission, and that is: the production of creative mould!

It is now industry's task to induce in its specialists, engineers, and doctors a sense of moral responsibility for the production of mould.

This sense of moral responsibility for the production of creative mould and critical weathering must be anchored in the laws dealing with education. +

+ Only those technologists and scientists who are capable of living in mould and creatively producing mould will be the masters of tomorrow. +

And only after things have been creatively covered in mould, from which we have much to learn, will a new and wonderful architecture come into being.

1958 Constant/Debord: Situationist definitions

In 1957 the amalgamation of the 'Lettriste Internationale' and the 'International Union for a Pictorial Bauhaus' gave birth to the 'Internationale Situationniste', which employed the concept 'Unitary Town Planning' as the slogan for its actions. The International Union for a Pictorial Bauhaus in turn was an act of protest against the first programme of the Hochschule für Gestaltung in Ulm formulated by Max Bill. (Gropius had authorized Bill to carry on the name 'Bauhaus' in connexion with the new establishment. Bill eventually forwent this.) The painter Asger Jorn set out his objections to Ulm in his book *Image and Form* (Milan 1954).

The following eleven points, which convey a brief definition of the Situationist action, are to be construed as a preparatory theme for the third conference of the International Situationists (I.S.)

1. The Situationists must at every opportunity combat retrogressive ideologies and forces, both in the field of culture and in particular wherever the question of the meaning of life is involved.

2. No one should regard his membership of the I.S. as merely an expression of his agreement in principle; it is desirable that the activity of all members be essentially in keeping with the goals worked out in common and with the need for disciplined action, both in practice and in public statements.

3. The possibility of unitary and collective creation is already being manifested through the disintegration of the individual arts. The I.S. cannot support an attempt to renew these arts.

4. The minimum programme of the I.S. includes both the striving for a perfect spatial art, which must extend to a unitary system of town planning, and the search for new modes of behaviour in conjunction with this spatial art.

5. Unitary town planning is determined by the uninterrupted complex activity through which man's environment is consciously recreated according to progressive plans in all domains.

6. The problems of living accommodation, transportation, and recreation can be solved only in conjunction with social, psychological, and artistic aspects of life, which accords with the hypothesis of the totality of the life style.

7. Unitary town planning – independently of all aesthetic considerations – is the result of a new kind of collective creation; and the development of this creative spirit is the precondition for a unitary town planning.

8. It is the immediate task of today's creatively active people to bring about conditions favourable to this development.

9. All means may be employed – provided they serve a unitary action. The co-ordination of artistic and scientific means must lead to complete fusion.

10. The creation of a situation means the creation of a transitory micro-world and – for a single moment in the life of a few – a play of events. It cannot be separated from the creation of a universal, relatively more lasting, environment by means of unitary town planning.

11. A created situation is a means for approaching unitary town planning, and unitary town planning is the indispensable basis for the creation – to be regarded both as a game and as a serious task – of the situation of a freer society.

Constant, Debord, Amsterdam, 10 November 1958

1960   William Katavolos:
Organics

The 'informal' painting and sculpture of the fifties were followed by ideas
concerning an 'informal' architecture. Again as in the twenties – at that time
with the idea of 'industrialized building' – there arose the call for new building
materials. We can look even farther back: as precisely as Paul Scheerbart
described and demanded the characteristics of our modern man-made
materials, so the American William Katavolos outlined in 1960 the
characteristics of a building material with which a 'Chemical Architecture'
could be realized. In this sense Katavolos – philosopher, lecturer, industrial
designer – claims a place in the ranks of the century's architect visionaries.

A new architecture is possible through the matrix of chemistry. Man must
stop making and manipulating, and instead allow architecture to happen.
There is a way beyond building just as the principles of waves, parabolas and
plummet lines exist beyond the mediums in which they form. So must architecture free itself from traditional patterns and become organic.

New discoveries in chemistry have led to the production of powdered and
liquid materials which when suitably treated with certain activating agents
expand to great size and then catalize and become rigid. We are rapidly gaining the necessary knowledge of the molecular structure of these chemicals,
together with the necessary techniques that will lead to the production of
materials which will have a specific programme of behaviour built into them
while still in the sub-microscopic stage. Accordingly it will be possible to take
minute quantities of powder and make them expand into predetermined
shapes, such as spheres, tubes, and toruses.

Visualize the new city grow moulded on the sea, of great circles of oil sub-
stances producing patterns in which plastics pour to form a network of strips
and discs that expand into toruses and spheres, and further perforate for many
purposes. Double walls are windowed in new ways containing chemicals to
heat, to cool, and to clean, ceiling patterns created like crystals, floors
formed like corals, surfaces structurally ornamented with visible stress patterns that leap weightlessly above us. The fixed floors provide the paraphern-
alia for living, a vast variety of disposable pods plugged into more permanent
cellular grids.

Let us discuss the principles of organics in how it might affect something as
simple and as complicated as a chair. To be comfortable a chair must vibrate,
must flex, must massage, must be high off the floor to allow for easy access or
vacation. It should be also low to the floor, when sitting, to take pressure off
those areas of the body which easily constrict. It must also be capable of
educating its occupant, of having sounds come stereophonically to his ears, it
must create correct ionic fields, it must have the ability to disappear when not
in use, and above all it must be beautiful. A chair like this does not exist. My
researches have led toward these needs again and again. We could create a

mechanical contrivance which would do all of these things, but from my own experience with such machines in which to sit, they would not fully satisfy or delight the eye of the beholder. Now this becomes very possible using blow moulded methods of plastics with a double wall, which could be filled with chemicals of various densities, which could allow the outside surface to be structurally ribbed in a beautiful pattern, which would allow the inner shell to flex and to receive the body, a chair which could rise through pressure to receive the sitter, then softly descend for closer contact with the floor, a chair which could easily again bring coolness or heat through chemical action, vibration and flex, a chair which could incorporate electronic devices for sound, and also for creating correct ionic fields. A chair which would be an affirmation of all that has gone before and that which is now necessary. This we can do without mechanics, organically in much the same manner as similar actions, such as respiration, peristalsis, pulse rhythms, occur in many natural forms.

Carrying the principle further from furniture into the idea of containers for food, for liquids, we find that again the double wall structurally ribbed on the outside, smooth on the inside, could eliminate the need for refrigeration by chemically cooling the product within, or when activated or opened such a container might then chemically cook the soup, provide the disposable bowl itself from which to drink, and thereby make the stove, the sinks for cleaning, and areas for storage unnecessary, as we know them.

Again the organic process creates an immense simplification and allows a great freedom for the positioning of areas within the environment. As in the case of the bath and showers we find the double-walled container, which would enclose the form to the neck and chemically steam the occupant, would clean the body and then dry it.

To carry the point further the individual could then create his own plastic fabrics by pouring them in pleasing patterns around the base of the pedestal, allowing it to catalize and harden into continuous containers to wear in new ways.

Let us discuss the chemically packaged lavatory which would rise to a comfortable height for the user, then slowly lower to provide the particular position that we have found to be best for total evacuation. Again the entire unit would rise through pressure and allow its occupant to comfortably withdraw from it, leaving the waste products to be chemically consumed and packaged, thus eliminating the needs for connective pipes. Having cut the umbilicus we find it possible to create the new house on any site in that it is chemically a complete organism in which to live, deriving strength from its surrounds.

Houses such as this would grow to certain sizes, subdivide or fuse for larger functions. Great vaults would be produced with parabolic jets that catalize on contact with the air. Exploding patterns of an instantaneous architecture of transformations into desired densities, into known directions, for calculated durations. In the morning suburbs might come together to create cities, and at night move like music to other moorings for cultural needs or to produce the socio-political patterns that the new life demands.

1960   Reinhard Gieselmann/Oswald Mathias Ungers: Towards a new architecture

The appeal launched by Gieselmann (b.1925 in Münster) and Ungers (b.1926 in Kaisersesch) shows that the professional image of the architect has become blurred. The architect is already being spoken of as though he existed to assist the technologist to carry out a task. Profitability, rationalization of the building process, obstructive building regulations, and technical innovations increasingly distract attention from formal problems. Naked functionalism is screened by an openwork façade. Salvation is awaited from the calculating machine. Building threatens to be simplified into a mechanical process. Programmes convertible into numbers and figures guarantee tidy results. The main human functions appear to be: protecting, converting, carrying, regulating=skin, organs, bones, brain. The first protests against this are now being raised.

Creative art is unthinkable without a spiritual clash with tradition. In this clash existing form must be smashed in order to find the pure expression of one's own time. Architecture, like every other art, serves the genius as a means of expressing his epoch and keeping a living development in motion.

Architecture is partial creation. But every creative process is art. It is entitled to the highest spiritual status.

Technology is the application of knowledge and experience. Technology and construction are aids to execution. Technology is not art.

Form is the expression of spiritual content.

If we pursue the methods of technological, functional 'architecture' the result will be uniformity. Architecture loses its expression when technological, functional methods are employed. The result is apartment blocks that look like schools, schools like administrative buildings and administrative buildings like factories. An empty scaffolding is hung in front of them. Form becomes interchangeable through the use of a mathematical, hence non-artistic schematism.

The resulting 'architecture' is the expression of a materialistic social order whose principles are the primacy of technology and equalization.

The relationship to the environment is established programmatically and hence without tension. This lack of vitality gives rise to a spiritual vacuum.

The vital clash between the active individual and his environment is replaced by spiritual enslavement through the dictatorship of methodology.

Freedom lives only in the individual's clash with reality and in recognition of personal inner responsibility towards place, time and man.

This freedom exists today only in a living democratic order. To employ materialistic methods within this libertarian order is conscienceless and a sign of irresponsibility or stupidity. Both mean at all times a serious threat and danger to man's personal development.

The task is to preserve freedom for the unfolding of the creative spirit.

What architecture desires is the perfect expression of content.

Architecture is a vital penetration of a multi-layered, mysterious, evolved and structured reality. Its creative function is to manifest the task by which it is confronted, to integrate itself into that which already exists, to introduce points of emphasis and rise above its surroundings. Again and again it demands recognition of the *genius loci* out of which it grows. Architecture is no longer a two-dimensional impression but is becoming experience of corporeal and spatial reality achieved by walking around and entering into.

Rigidity is being replaced by movement, symmetry by asymmetry, statics by dynamics.

Monotonous obviousness is being replaced by surprise.

The essential viewpoint is from inside, not from outside.

The subject–object relationship has been done away with.

Architecture is the enveloping and sheltering of the individual, and hence a ful- filment and a deepening.

With this manifesto we address ourselves to all who are striving for a renewal of European architecture on this foundation.

1960 GEAM:
Programme for a mobile architecture

At the end of 1957 young architects from France, Holland, Poland, and Israel met in Paris as a 'groupe d'études d'architecture mobile' (GEAM). The last meeting of CIAM before its final dissolution – CIAM X in Dubrovnik in 1956 – had among other things raised questions of mobility, interconnexions, communication: questions that are being rendered increasingly urgent by the explosive development of big cities and conurbations. GEAM set itself the task of working out proposals for solving these problems. The first working conference took place in March 1958 in Rotterdam. This conference was also attended by architects from Germany.

A. The catastrophic difficulties of modern town planning are the outcome of a series of factors that may be characterized as follows:

1. Existing constructions and those still being put up today are too rigid and difficult to adapt to life as it is lived.
2. The growth of the population is unpredictable and cannot be planned for.
3. Traffic is increasing beyond all bounds.
4. Property rights are outdated and patterns of ownership have in many cases become petrified.
5. The price of dwelling units is too high.
6. There is an ever-increasing discrepancy between town and town planning on the one hand and the rapid advance of science and technology on the other.

B. The daily life of the population is suffering as a result of these conditions. This may be seen from the following phenomena:

1. Traffic is congested and at certain times of day comes almost to a stop.
2. Dwellings have to some extent become brick prisons for families.
3. The weekend flight into the open air is constantly assuming greater proportions.
4. The rhythm of the individual's life is imposed upon him and it is virtually impossible to mould one's own environment.
5. A great number of city dwellers feel lonely and isolated.
6. Neighbourhoods have come into being entirely haphazard and remain difficult to influence.

C. For the general improvement of these conditions GEAM has established certain principles and makes the following proposals:

1. Reform of property rights in building land and air space with a view to achieving easier interchange. Introduction of a system of stratified utilization of air space by the inhabitants.
2. Constructions should be variable and interchangeable.
3. The spatial units produced by these constructions should likewise be alterable and interchangeable in their use.
4. The inhabitants must be given the opportunity to adapt their dwellings themselves to the needs of the moment.
5. Industry and prefabrication must be utilized to the full in the manufacture of the constructions as a means of lowering prices.
6. Town and town planning must be capable of adaptation to the development of traffic.
7. Residential and work places, as well as areas for physical and spiritual culture, must be intermingled throughout the individual sections of the city.

D. In order to put the aforementioned principles into practice, GEAM proposes elaboration of the following techniques:

1. Development of variable and interchangeable elements of construction, as for example:
   (a) exterior walls,
   (b) interior walls,
   (c) movable floors and ceilings.
2. Development of easily altered means of supplying buildings with power and water and the disposal of garbage.
3. Development of larger town-creating spatial units, such as:
   (a) interchangeable containers (travelling, flying, floating),
   (b) buildings on rafts,
   (c) buildings bridging over spaces,
   (d) air-conditioned open spaces.

Paris, 5 April 1960
David George Emmerich, Camille Frieden, Yona Friedman, Günter Günschel, Jean Pierre Pecquet, Werner Ruhnau

As a supplement to the 1960 programme, the statement of March 1961 reads: An optimal distribution of elements in town planning is made possible by the mobility of component parts. This will lead to the reintegration of those functions that have become divided. Multifunctionality of the urban organism will reduce the problems of communication.
This principle will render the problem of static form outmoded.
Structures and regulations regarding use must be planned.

1960 Louis I. Kahn: Order is

At the end of the fifties there began in the United States a slow process of replacement. The great German architects of the interwar years, the influential teachers of architecture in America in the thirties and forties – Breuer, Gropius, Hilberseimer, Mies van der Rohe, Moholy-Nagy, Wachsmann, Wagner – if they were still alive, gradually retired from their teaching posts. Younger men took their place. The architectural departments of the less well-known universities began to attract attention. Louis I. Kahn (b.1901 on the island of Ösel, Estonia) taught at Yale and the University of Pennsylvania. He told his students: 'A good question is greater than the most brilliant answer.'

Design is form-making in order
Form emerges out of a system of construction
Growth is a construction
In **order** is creative force
In **design** is the means – where with what when with how much
The nature of space reflects what it wants to be
        Is the auditorium a Stradivarius
                or an ear
        Is the auditorium a creative instrument
            keyed to Bach or Bartók
            played by the conductor
            or is it a conventional hall
In the nature of space is the spirit and the will to exist a certain way
        Design must closely follow that will
        Therefore a stripe-painted horse is not a zebra
        Before a railroad station is a building
        it wants to be a street
        it grows out of the needs of street
            out of the order of movement
        A meeting of contours englazed.
Through the **nature** – why
Through the **order** – what
Through **design** – how
A form emerges from the structural elements inherent in the form.
        A dome is not conceived when questions arise how to build it.
        Nervi grows an arch
        Fuller grows a dome
Mozart's compositions are designs
        They are exercises of order – intuitive
        Design encourages more designs
        Designs derive their imagery from order
        Imagery is the memory – the form

Style is an adopted order
The same **order** created the elephant and created man
They are different designs
Begun from different aspirations
Shaped from different circumstances
Order does not imply Beauty
The same order created the dwarf and Adonis
Design is not making Beauty
Beauty emerges from selection
affinities
integration
love
Art is a form-making life in order – psychic
Order is intangible
It is a level of creative consciousness
forever becoming higher in level
The higher the order the more diversity in design
Order supports integration
From what the space wants to be the unfamiliar may be revealed to the architect.
From order he will derive creative force and power of self-criticism to give form to this unfamiliar.
Beauty will evolve.

1960 Werner Ruhnau/Yves Klein: Project for an aerial architecture

In 1923 *G* demanded: 'Economy. Pure relationship of strength and material.'
In forty years the demand had lost none of its fascination. Bruno Taut's phrase concerning the 'light point' that had to be found was topical as never before. Buckminster Fuller asked: What does a building weigh? Lightweight structures were conquering a still limitless field. Fluid and gaseous materials were used in construction. A new sensibility was developing. The architect Werner Ruhnau (b. 1922 in Königsberg) and the painter Yves Klein (Le Monochrome) wanted to found a 'school of sensibility'. *ZERO* proclaimed: 'We live, we are for everything'. Ruhnau and Klein were for a life in aerial architecture.

'In our minds aerial architecture was always merely a stage that is proposed today for the air-conditioning of privileged geographical spaces.'

We propose protecting a city by a roof of moving air. A central motorway leads to the airport, dividing the city in two: a residential quarter and a quarter for work, industry and mechanical devices. The roof of air simultaneously air-conditions and protects the privileged space.

A floor of transparent glass. Storage underground (kitchens, bathrooms, store-rooms and production plant).

The concept of secrecy, which is still known to us, will have vanished from this city flooded with light and completely open to the outside world. A new condition of human intimacy will exist. The inhabitants live naked. The former patriarchal family system will no longer exist. The community will be complete, free, individual, impersonal. The inhabitants' main occupation: leisure.

The obstacles that used to be regarded in architecture as troublesome necessities will have become luxuries: fire-walls, water-walls, forms carried by the air, fire-fountains, water-fountains, swimming baths, air beds, air seats . . . The real goal of immaterial architecture: the air-conditioning of large geographical dwelling areas.

This air-conditioning will be achieved not so much through technological miracles as essentially through a transformation of human sensibility into a function of the cosmos. The theory of 'immaterialization' negates the spirit of fictitious science.

Through evolved sensibility, 'a new dimension, guided by the spirit', the climate and the spiritual conditions on the surfaces of our earth will in future be transformed.

'To want means to invent.' To this wanting is added the will to live what one has invented, and the miracle will be accomplished in all the realms of nature. Ben-Gurion: 'He who does not believe in miracles is not a realist.'

1960 'Situationists':
International Manifesto

> Debord, one of the spokesmen of the 'Situationists', wrote in 1957: 'Unitary town planning is defined first through the application of the totality of the arts and technologies as partnered forces in an integral composition of the environment . . . Further, unitary town planning is dynamic, that is to say in close relationship to life style and behaviour. The element to which everything is ultimately reduced is not the house, but the architectonic complex, which is the unification of all those factors that determine an environment or a series of impinging environments . . . Architecture must advance by taking as its subject exciting situations rather than exciting forms.'

A new human force, which the existing framework of society will not be able to suppress, is growing day by day along with the irresistible development of technology and the frustration of its potential applications in our meaningless social life.

Alienation and oppression in society cannot be mastered in any of their specific manifestations, but simply rejected *en bloc* along with this society itself. All real progress is clearly dependent upon a revolutionary solution of the crisis of the present time in all its forms.

What are the prospects for the organization of life in a society which, genuinely, 'will reorganize production on the foundations of a free and equal association of producers'? Automation of production and socialization of essential goods will increasingly reduce work as an external necessity and will finally give the individual complete freedom. Thus freed from all economic responsibility, freed from all his debts and guilt towards the past and other people, man will dispose of a new surplus value, impossible to calculate in money terms because it cannot be reduced to the measurement of paid work: the value of play, of life freely constructed. The exercise of this playful creativity is the guarantee of the freedom of each and all, within the framework of that equality which is guaranteed by the absence of exploitation of one man by another. The freedom to play means man's creative autonomy, *which goes beyond the old division between imposed work and passive leisure.*

The Church used to burn those whom it called sorcerers in order to repress the primitive tendencies to play preserved in popular festivals. In the society that is at present dominant, which mass-produces wretched pseudo-games devoid of participation, any true artistic activity is necessarily classified as criminal. It remains semi-clandestine and comes to light as scandal.

What exactly is the situation? The need is for the realization of a higher game, more precisely a stimulus to this game known as human existence. Revolutionary players from every country can unite in the I.S. in order to start emerging from the prehistoric phase of daily living.

From now on, we propose an autonomous organization of the producers of the new culture, independent of existing political and trade union organizations, because we do not credit them with the ability to do more than organize what already exists.

The most urgent aim which we set this organization, at the moment when it is emerging from its initial experimental phase to embark upon its first public campaign, is to capture UNESCO. The bureaucratization of art and the whole of culture, unified on a world scale, is a new phenomenon that expresses the profound relationship between the social systems coexisting in the world, on the basis of eclectic conservation and the reproduction of the past. The retort of revolutionary artists to these new conditions must be a new type of action. As the very existence of this directorial concentration, localized in a single building, favours seizure by means of a *coup*; and as the institution is totally destitute of any possibility of meaningful use outside our subversive perspectives, we feel justified before our contemporaries in seizing this apparatus. And we shall seize it. We are resolved to take possession of UNESCO, even if only for a little while, because we are confident of promptly achieving significant results that will continue to light the way during a long period of heavy demands.

What will be the principal characteristics of the new culture, first of all by comparison with the old art?

As opposed to spectacle, Situationist culture, when put into practice, will introduce total participation.

As opposed to the preservation of art, it will involve direct organization of the lived moment.

As opposed to divided art, it will be a global practice relating simultaneously to all usable elements. It tends naturally towards collective and no doubt anonymous production (at least to the extent that, since works *will not be stockpiled like articles of merchandise*, this culture will not be dominated by the need to leave a mark). Its experiments offer, at the very least, a revolution in behaviour and a unitary dynamic town planning capable of taking in the whole planet and being subsequently extended to all habitable planets.

As opposed to unilateral art, Situationist culture will be an art of dialogue, an art of interaction. Artists – together with the whole of visible culture – have come to be entirely separated from society, as they are separated among themselves by competition. But even before this impasse brought about by capitalism, art was essentially unilateral, without reply. It will pass beyond this era of primitive enclosedness and attain total communication.

Since at a higher stage everyone will become an artist – that is to say, both producer and consumer of a total cultural achievement – we shall see the rapid dissolution of the linear criterion of novelty. Since everyone will be, so to speak, a Situationist, we shall see a multidimensional plethora of new trends, of experiments, of 'schools', all radically different, and this *no longer in succession but simultaneously*.

We shall now inaugurate what will be, historically speaking, the last of all professions. The role of the Situationist, the amateur-expert, the anti-specialist, will remain a form of specialization until the moment of economic and mental abundance when everyone will become an 'artist' in a sense which artists have never before achieved – in the sense that everyone will construct his own life. However, the last profession in history is so close to the society without permanent division of labour that when it appears within the I.S. it is generally denied the characteristics of a profession.

To those who do not properly understand us, we say with utter contempt: 'The Situationists, of whom you perhaps believe yourselves to be the judges, will one day judge you. We await you at the turning-point that will mean the inevitable liquidation of the world of privation in all its forms. These are our aims, and they will be the future aims of humanity.'

1960   Eckhard Schulze-Fielitz:
The Space City

When Wachsmann published his works on spatial building systems in September 1954 he gained many adherents. New systems were devised and especially new applications. From the possibility of so enlarging the hollow spaces of these bearing structures that the sum of all the hollow spaces approached the volume of the total bearing structure Schulze-Fielitz (b. 1929 in Stettin) evolved the idea of a variable, internally 'mobile' system of town planning, which within and together with the spatial grid could grow or vanish in accordance with the needs of the population. Yona Friedman (b. 1923 in Budapest) projected such space cities into the air space above the old, no longer functioning settlements (see page 183).

As a result of the machine's ability to multiply and the rapidly increasing population figures, our age has acquired a dynamic trend towards mass production; the need is quantity and quality with the minimum effort. But a raised standard of living through standardization seems dearly bought with the growing monotony of our industrially manufactured environment and restriction of freedom of decision. The ever-growing army of machines and automata will relieve man of an ever-increasing proportion of manual labour; electronic brains are taking over intellectual drudgery. But machines manufacture serial products, elements, and we shall have to tell them which elements, we shall have to test their capacity for combination. New materials will demand new systems of combination.

The systematization of space is a precondition for the spatial combination of standardized parts and hence a basic principle of prefabrication.

Despite rigid systematization, spatial modular co-ordination offers great freedom of choice and arrangement and hence a synthesis of the only apparently mutually exclusive tendencies of mass production and individual multiplicity. Interchangeability of spatially co-ordinated quanta offers flexibility and adaptation in dynamic developments. Serial building will be influenced by geometry, topology, group theory and the principles of combination.

The space structure is a macro-material capable of modulation, analogous to an intellectual model in physics, according to which the wealth of phenomena can be reduced to a few elementary particles. The physical material is a discontinuum of whole-number units, molecules, atoms, elementary particles. Their combinational possibilities determine the characteristics of the material.

It is modulation of the spatial structure according to kind, size, material, and position that permits us to take the daring step of presenting it as a comprehensive means of town planning. The space city is a discontinuous continuum, discontinuous through the demarcation between the part and the whole, continuous through the unalterable possibilities of alteration. In a free society the perfect planning of a city is neither possible nor desirable; it means fixation that impedes unpredictable developments.

The space city, on the other hand, is an agglomeration of various spatial structures in pursuance of development; the ductus of the structure steers the unavoidable proliferation into ordered channels; freedom lies in the infinite possibilities of combination.

When the details are suitably designed, co-ordination of measurement permits the mutual interchange of all parts. This makes possible solution of the basic dilemma between the dynamic of urban life and the static of the built structure. Electronic calculating centres will examine the static and organizational conditions calling for change: automatic factories will produce the material substance of the city.

Multi-storey inhabited spatial carrying structures will bridge over great spans by their static height. In the centres of density the city will rise up from the ground, leaving the latter to mechanical transport. The possibility of greater density, building over traffic areas and watercourses, keeping whole stretches free for flowing or stationary traffic, the strict segregation of types of traffic, make possible solution of the problems of circulation in centres of traffic concentration. The smallest possible number of obstacles stand in the way of traffic and its unforeseeable development, thereby avoiding from the outset the majority of the problems we face today. On the other hand, the space city creates a continuous, three-dimensional public space which was lost when the motor-car perverted streets and squares into motorways and parking lots.

A three-dimensional system of co-ordinates identical with a spatial grid will facilitate organization and orientation in the space city, yet the multiplicity of the possible material forms it can take leaves room for individuality and anarchy. Thanks to the ordering of space, the architectural substance is adaptable to every topographical datum, absorbing, altering, levelling, or raising it.

The space city accompanies the profile of the landscape as a crystalline layer; it is itself a landscape, comparable to geological formations with peaks and valleys, ravines and plateaux, comparable to the leafy area of the forest with its branches. To regenerate existing cities, structures will stretch above their degenerate sections and cause them to fall into disuse.

Consistency of these ideas demands that property or exploitation rights shall no longer – in pursuance of the agricultural tradition – be related to the surface area (as the medium of agricultural production) but to utilizable space. The compact city offers possibilities of an improved heating economy, a self-air-conditioning; in the future it will even permit a controlled internal climate of the city, which could radically reduce the cost of insulating the individual building. The space city is the structural, systematized, prefabricated, growing or shrinking, adaptable, air-conditioned, multi-purpose space labyrinth that can be fitted together or taken apart at will.

1960 Constant: New Babylon (excerpt)

Up to 1953, Constant (Nieuwenhuys) (b.1920 in Amsterdam) was a painter. At this juncture, he states: 'The picture of the world changed; mechanized, technoid environments emerged. But the artist stood aside, was obviously incapable of participating in the process.' Constant roamed through Paris and London, observed each city and its construction. He recognized agglomeration as an artistic medium. 'Demain la poésie logera la vie' was henceforth his theme. In 1956 he met Asger Jorn and Debord and developed with them the first plans for 'unitary town planning'. But their standpoints quickly diverged. Constant began his story of New Babylon.

Individualist culture is at an end, its institutions are exhausted. The present task of the artist can only be to prepare the way for a future mass culture. For if there is still to be any talk of culture it will have to carry a mass society, and then the means can be sought only within mechanization. The shaping of the material environment and the liberation and organization of everyday life are the points of departure for new cultural forms. My *New Babylon project* arose as an illustrative sketch and elaboration of these ideas. It is the *experimental thought and play model* for the establishment of principles for a new and different culture.

New Babylon is not primarily a town planning project. Equally, it is not intended as a work of art in the traditional sense nor as an example of architectonic structure.

New Babylon in its present form may be construed as a proposal, as an attempt to give material shape to the theory of unitary town planning, to maintain a creative game with an imaginary environment that is set in place of the inadequate, unsatisfying environment of contemporary life.

The modern city is dead; it has fallen victim to utility. New Babylon is a project for a city in which it is possible to live. And to live means to be creative.

New Babylon is the object of a mass creativity; it reckons with the activation of the enormous creative potential which, now unused, is present in the masses. It reckons with the disappearance of non-creative work as the result of automation; it reckons with the transformation of morality and thought, it reckons with a new social organization.

But it also reckons with facts like the rapid spread of the world population, the perpetual growth of traffic, the cultivation of the whole planet, and total urbanization. Thus the project takes account of the purely functional problems of current town planning, traffic and housing and strives for extreme solutions. But its main theme is a new regard for social space. It is the medium for a new creativity that is to manifest itself in daily life, by means of a continually varied arrangement of the environment, in harmony with a dynamic way of life. In a technical respect, it is a simple, thoroughly structured framework, a scaffolding set on pillars and raised up *in toto* from the ground. Thus the ground is left at the free disposal of traffic.

Division of the scaffolding into smaller units (sectors), each 5 to 10 hectares large, gives rise to a complicated, netlike pattern interspersed by remnants of landscape and crisscrossed by a traffic grid, which can run independently of the built-up area.

On the raised platform, dwelling and social space form a vast coherent edifice which, in all its several storeys, is artificially air-conditioned and lit. The upper terrace, the 'roof', can include sports areas and airports.

Apart from dwelling quarters, the interior of these sectional buildings consists of a large public space serving the purposes of social life. It is divided up by means of movable walls and constructional parts into variable volumes that can be linked by a play of stairs, platforms and corridors. This gives rise to a multiplicity of different ambiences that can be altered at any given moment. The character can be influenced and determined by an abundant manipulation of colour, sound, light, climate, by the use of the most varied kinds of technical apparatus, and by psychological procedures. The shaping of the interior at any given moment, the interplay of the various environments takes place in harmony with the experimental life-play of the inhabitants. The city brings about a dynamically active, creative unfolding of life.

One can wander for prolonged periods through the interconnected sectors, entering into the adventure afforded by this unlimited labyrinth. The express traffic on the ground and the helicopters over the terraces cover great distances, making possible a spontaneous change of location.

The function of dwelling is adapted to this adventurous and dynamic life. It can scarcely be planned any longer to cater for permanent dwelling. The dwelling spaces, as parts of the rest of the interior space above which they are scattered, are best regarded as a kind of residential hotel in a non-commercial sense, favouring frequent change of domicile.

Such a project is dependent upon sociological, psychological, scientific, technological, organizational, and artistic factors.

Already at this Utopian stage a collective collaboration of the most varied interests is an inescapable condition.

But New Babylon will first be realized by its inhabitants.

1961 R. Buckminster Fuller:
The architect as world planner (excerpt)

On the occasion of the congress of the International Union of Architects in London in 1961 Richard Buckminster Fuller spoke on the task of the architect in the present world situation. As thirty years before, Fuller developed a planning programme that was to span the entire world. He projected the idea of a world in which the means of existence had been made completely available to mankind. The architect, he said, must become a world planner who has arrived at a fixed hierarchy of processes in the world and on the basis of this hierarchy practises world town planning with all the scientific aids at his disposal.

... I propose that the architectural departments of all the universities around the world be encouraged by the UIA to invest the next ten years in a continuing problem of how to make the total world's resources serve 100% of humanity through competent design.

The general theory of education at present starts students off with elementary components and gradually increases the size of the complex of components with which the student will be concerned. The scheme is to go from the particular towards the whole but seems never to reach the whole. In many of the architectural schools the first-year student is given a problem in terms of a country town and has to plan and design the buildings for that country town. The next year he must do a larger town, a small industrial town. In the third year he is engaged in a large industrial city, and in his fourth year he is engaged with larger cities, such as London or New York. The schools never reach out to national, let alone world problems. Local town planning is almost everywhere invalidated by the sweep of world events. The automobile highway cloverleaf programmes are inadequate to the concept of total man being advantaged with his own vehicle; parking problems continually frustrate and negate the too-local horizon of town planning.

The first year's total world planning by the students and its designed implementation may be expected to disclose great amateurishness and inadequacies, but not only will the criticism come from the architectural profession, it will also be evoked from the politicos, from the economists, the industrialists, excited by its treading on their doorsteps, out of which criticism the next year's round of world designing by the students may be greatly advantaged. The second, third, and fourth years should show swift acceleration in the comprehension of the problem and the degree of satisfaction of the problem.

The world planning by the students must be predicated upon the concept of first things first, upon a scheduled hierarchy of events.

The comprehensive world resources data now exist in a number of establishments, but is primarily available to all the universities of the world through UNESCO. What UNESCO does not have, it is in a good position to direct the researcher to successfully acquire.

At the present moment in history, what is spoken of as foreign policy by the respective nations consists essentially of their plans to bring about conditions which would uniquely foster their respective unique kinds of survival in the Malthusian 'you or me-ness'.* For any one of the foreign policies of any of the nations or groups of nations to become a world plan, would mean that approximately half of the world's nations would have to surrender, and would mean the development of a highly biased plan as applied to the whole. In the nature of political compromises, it is logical to assume that the foreign policy of any one nation will never succeed in satisfying comprehensive world planning.

It is clearly manifest, however, in this Sixth Congress of the International Union of Architects that the architects are able to think regarding such world planning in a manner transcendental to any political bias. My experience around the world and amongst the students tells me that the students themselves tend always to transcend political bias and that all of them are concerned with the concept of making the world work through competent design.

In much investigation and enquiry I have had no negative response to the programme of organization of the student capability to the raising of the performance of the world resources to serve 100% of humanity by peaceful, comprehensive laboratory experiment and progressive design evolution.

It is probable that if the architectural students are progressively disciplined to breadth of capability in chemistry, physics, mathematics, bio-chemistry, psychology, economics, and industrial technology, that they will swiftly and ably penetrate the most advanced scientific minds resident in the university, and as their programmes evolve from year to year in improving capability, that the students will be able to bring the highest integral scientific resources of man to bear upon their solutions of world town planning and its design instrumentation and operational regeneration.

The next Congress should then be almost completely preoccupied with reviewing all such inventories and plans – with this first stocktaking of what man has to do, and what he has to do it with! What will appear will unquestionably be world news of the first order, and not only world news but the news that men all around the Earth have waited for. The common goals for all to work toward will be reduced from empty words to simple physical objectives.

* Malthus, the British economist, 1766–1834. Malthus proved that the population of the Earth increases in geometrical progression, the food supply only in arithmetical progression.

1962 Walter Pichler/Hans Hollein: Absolute architecture

Absolute architecture – 'human beings are now merely tolerated in its domain'. This proposition by Walter Pichler (b.1936 in Ponte Nova) is the most absolute thesis in the architectural manifestoes of our century. For absolute means detached. Means here: detached from history, detached from deeds, detached from thought. And absolute architecture means here: architecture freed from its object, man; non-objective architecture. The chain of adventures undergone by those who set out in this century to learn a new architecture ends in the totally uncommitted phenomenon of an 'Absolute Architecture'. It is, adds Hans Hollein (b.1934 in Vienna), purposeless.

Architecture. It is born of the most powerful thoughts. For men it will be a compulsion, they will stifle in it or they will live – live, as I mean the word. Architecture is not an integument for the primitive instincts of the masses. Architecture is an embodiment of the power and longings of a few men. It is a brutal affair that has long since ceased to make use of art. It has no consideration for stupidity and weakness. It never serves. It crushes those who cannot bear it. Architecture is the law of those who do not believe in the law but make it. It is a weapon. Architecture ruthlessly employs the strongest means at its disposal at any given moment. Machines have taken possession of it and human beings are now merely tolerated in its domain.

Walter Pichler

Architecture is a spiritual order, realized through building.

Architecture – an idea built into infinite space, manifesting man's spiritual energy and power, the material form and expression of his destiny, of his life. From its origins until today the essence and meaning of architecture have not changed. To build is a basic human need. It is first manifested not in the putting up of protective roofs, but in the erection of sacred structures, in the indication of focal points of human activity – the beginning of the city.

All building is religious.

Architecture – the expression of man himself – at once flesh and spirit.

Architecture is elemental, sensual, primitive, brutal, terrible, mighty, dominating.

But it is also the embodiment of the most subtle emotions, a sensitive record of the most refined sensations, a materialization of the spiritual.

Architecture is not the satisfaction of the needs of the mediocre, is not an environment for the petty happiness of the masses. Architecture is made by those who stand at the highest level of culture and civilization, at the peak of their epoch's development. Architecture is an affair of the élite. Architecture – space – determines with the means of building. Architecture dominates space.

Dominates it by shooting up into the heights; it hollows out the earth, projects and soars far above the ground, spreads in all directions. Dominates it through mass and through emptiness. Dominates space through space.

This architecture is not a matter of beauty. If we desire beauty at all, it is not so much beauty of form, of proportion, as a sensual beauty of elemental force.

The shape of a building does not evolve out of the material conditions of a purpose. A building ought not to display its utilitarian function, is not the expression of structure and construction, is not a covering or a refuge. A building is itself.

Architecture is purposeless.

What we build will find its utilization.

Form does not follow function. Form does not arise of its own accord. It is the great decision of man to make a building as a cube, a pyramid or a sphere.

Form in architecture is determined by the individual, is built form.

Today, for the first time in human history, at this point in time when an immensely advanced science and perfected technology offer us all possible means, we build what and how we will, we make an architecture that is not determined by technology but utilizes technology, a pure, absolute architecture.

Today man is master over infinite space.

Hans Hollein

1962 Yona Friedman:
The ten principles of space town planning

1. The future of towns: they will be centres of leisure, of entertainment, centres of public life, centres of organization and of decisions of public interest. The other functions (work, production) will be more and more automated and consequently, less and less linked to the great agglomerations. The raw material 'worker' will lose its importance and be transformed into 'spectator' or 'client'.

2. The new society of towns must not be influenced by the town planner. Social distinctions between the different quarters must be spontaneous. A surplus of about 10% is sufficient for the inhabitants to be able to choose their respective quarters according to their social preferences.

3. The big cities must be able to contain, in place of industry, agriculture. The urban peasant is a social necessity.

4. Towns must be air-conditioned. The air-conditioning of towns permits a greater freedom and a greater efficacy as to usage: the streets become centres of public life.

5. The buildings which collectively form the physical town must be on a level with modern technology (today's bridges, for example, are often several miles long).

6. A new town 'risen from the desert' is not generally viable. Big cities come into existence through the development of former small towns: the big city must be the intensification of existing towns.

7. The three-dimensional technique of town planning (spatial town planning) permits the grouping of quarters both juxtaposed and superimposed.

8. The buildings that make up towns must be skeletons that can be filled at will. The fitting out of the skeletons will depend upon the initiative of each inhabitant.

9. We do not know the optimum size of a town. In any case, experience shows that towns with fewer than three million inhabitants relapse into provincialism, towns with more than this number become gigantic. Therefore a limit of three million inhabitants seems empirically to be the optimum size.

10. Foreseeing a tendency for the population to gravitate towards the cities, it is no exaggeration to estimate that in the near future cities will contain

80–85% of humanity (instead of 50% as at present). Hence the large agglomeration that has the advantage socially (entertainments) and technically (air-conditioning, transport) will win the day over other types of agglomeration. It is no exaggeration to imagine the whole of France contained in ten to twelve cities of 3,000,000 inhabitants, the whole of Europe in 100 to 120 cities, the whole of China in 200 cities and the whole world agglomerated in 1000 big cities.

1963   **We demand**

From the exhibition 'Heimat, Deine Häuser' in Stuttgart, June 1963

From the state	new land regulations ensuring for town planning the right of disposal over land ownership in areas of concentration; a change in the laws governing building assistance.
From the province	decisive participation by progressive planners and architects in formulating the new provincial building regulations.
From the municipalities	independent planning, freed from romantic prejudices and chance boundaries of ownership, independent architects as planners, more planning competitions.
From the building societies	better designed dwellings through the employment of better architects, support for planning, recognition and assumption of cultural responsibilities.
From property owners	more consideration for the public interest, less self-interest, understanding and openness towards planning.
From the architects	consciousness of the artistic task of architecture, more consideration of the social, economic and technological developments connected with their work, elimination from the profession of the evils of brokerage and speculation.
From the universities	participation in public problems, so that their research work may be acknowledged and utilized.
From the press	more space for the needs of planning and habitation, more criticism and enlightenment instead of mere factual reports.
From the surveyors' offices	collaboration in the realization of new forms of dwelling and estate layout, separation of the legal and technical aspects, unbureaucratic fulfilment of their tasks, decisions on questions

of form in conjunction with independent architects, people not to be prevented from obtaining better housing by outdated laws and outmoded principles.

Max Bächer, Wilfried Beck-Erlang, Walter Belz, Siegfried Hieber, Hans Kammerer, Hans Luz, Werner Luz, Gerhard Schwab.

Sources

Figures on the left refer to the pages in this book on which each extract appears. Where a number of extracts have the same source bibliographical details are given only for the first entry, and figures in square brackets refer to these entries.

13 *Notizen von einer Reise nach Griechenland*, Wagner, Weimar 1905. Reprinted in *Vom Neuen Stil*, Leipzig 1907. Quoted from *Zum Neuen Stil* (the writings of Van de Velde selected and edited by Hans Curjel), R. Piper & Co. Verlag, Munich 1955, p. 139 f.

14 *Das Deutsche Kunstgewerbe 1906*, Verlag F. Bruckmann, Munich 1906. Quoted from *Lesebuch für Baumeister*, Karl H. Henssel Verlag, Berlin 1947, p.416 ff.

18 *Vom Neuen Stil*, Insel Verlag, Leipzig 1907. Quoted from [9], p.150.

19 *Trotzdem 1900–1930*, Brenner Verlag, Innsbruck 1931. Quoted from *Adolf Loos, Sämtliche Schriften*, edited by Franz Glück, Vol. I, Verlag Herold, Vienna–Munich 1962, p.276 ff.

25 'Die Souveränität des Einzelnen', foreword to *Ausgeführte Bauten und Entwürfe*, Verlag E. Wasmuth, Berlin 1910. Quoted from *Frank Lloyd Wright, Writings and Buildings*, edited by Edgar Kaufmann and Ben Raeburn, copyright 1960, by permission of the publisher, Horizon Press, New York, p.102 f.

26 Address given at the annual meeting of the Deutscher Werkbund in Dresden 1911. Quoted from the *Jahrbuch des Deutschen Werkbundes 1912*, Jena 1912, p.18 f.

28 Quoted from *Bauwelt*, Ullstein, Berlin 1962, Number 27, p.770 f.

32 *Glasarchitektur*, Verlag Der Sturm, Berlin 1914.

34 *L'Architettura*, Rome 1956, Number 13, p.516 f.

39 *De Stijl*, II, Number 1, November 1918, p.2. Quoted from *konkrete kunst*, exhibition catalogue, Zürich (Helmhaus) 1960, p.15.

41 Pamphlet. Reprinted in Conrads/Sperlich, *Phantastische Architektur*, Verlag Gerd Hatje, Stuttgart 1960, p.135 f.

44 Pamphlet, in the author's possession.

46 Pamphlet. See also [38], p. 137 f.

49 Hans M. Wingler, *The Bauhaus*, MIT Press, Cambridge, Massachusetts, p.31 ff.

54 Erich Mendelsohn, *Das Gesamtschaffen des Architekten*, Rudolf Mosse Buchverlag, Berlin 1930, p.7 ff.

56   *Gabo, Konstruktive Plastik*, exhibition catalogue from the Kestner-Gesellschaft, Hanover 1930.

57   *Frühlicht* 1920. Compare new impression 1963 in *Bauwelt Fundamente*, Vol.8, p.11.

59   *Vers une architecture*, Paris 1923. Quoted from *Towards a new architecture*, London 1927, p.7 ff.

63   *Frühlicht 1921*. Compare new impression 1963 in *Bauwelt Fundamente*, Vol.8, p.69

64   *De Stijl*, V, p.62, Rotterdam 1922.

66   *De Stijl*, catalogue 81, Stedelijk Museum, Amsterdam 1951, p.16.

67   *De Stijl*, VI, p.89.

69   See above [47], p.65 f.

71   *'G' Material zur elementaren Gestaltung*, Berlin, July 1923.

72   See above [51], p.22 ff.

74   See above [67].

76   *Das Kunstblatt*, edited by Paul Westheim, Kiepenheuer, Potsdam 1923, Numbers 11/12.

78   *De Stijl*, XII, 6/7, Rotterdam 1924.

81   *'G,'* Number 3, Berlin 1924.

83   *Wendingen*, Amsterdam 1924, Number 3.

87   *Suprematismus – Die gegenstandslose Welt*, DuMont Dokumente, Cologne 1962, p.283 ff. Also available in English as *The Non-objective World*, Chicago 1959.

89   *Urbanisme*, Paris 1925.

95   See above [47], p. 109 f.

98   *De Stijl*. Quoted from *'G'*, Berlin 1926, Number IV (March).

99   *Almanach de l'Architecture moderne*, Paris 1926.

102   *Die Form*, 2nd year 1927, Number 2, p.59.

103   *Bauwelt*, Ullstein, Berlin 1927, Number 49, p.1211 ff.

106   *Russland—Europa—Amerika*, Rudolf Mosse Buchverlag, Berlin 1929, p.217.

109   *Das neue Frankfurt*, 1928, p.195 f.

114   Pamphlet, appeared 1928 in the international review *'i 10'*.

115 'ABC', *Beiträge zum Bauen*, 2nd series, Basle 1927/28, Number 4, p.1.

117 *bauhaus, Zeitschrift für Gestaltung*, 2nd year, Dessau 1928. Quoted from [47], p. 153 f.

121 'Russland–Rekonstruktion der Architektur in der Sowjetunion,' *Neues Bauen in der Welt I*, Vienna 1930, p.38 ff.

123 *Die Form*, 5th year, Number 15, 1.8.1930, p.406, and 7th year, Number 10, 15.10.1932, p.306.

124 'To the Young Man in Architecture', in Frank Lloyd Wright, *The Future of Architecture*, copyright 1953, by permission of the publisher, Horizon Press, New York, p. 215 ff.

126 *Innendekoration*, 37th year, Alexander Koch, Stuttgart 1932.

128 *T-Square*, Philadelphia, February 1932.

137 *Charte d'Athènes*, Paris 1942, reprinted Paris 1957.

146 Extracted from 'A Program for City Reconstruction', in *The Architectural Forum*, New York, July 1943 (Copyright 1943 by Whitney Publications, Inc.)

148 *Baukunst und Werkform*, 1st year, Number 1, Heidelberg 1947, p.29.

150 *Le Surréalisme en 1947*, International exhibition of Surrealism, Paris 1947, p.131 ff.

152 *Werk*, Winterthur 1949, Number 8. Quoted from [9], p.244 ff.

154 Quoted from Philip Johnson, *Mies van der Rohe*, Museum of Modern Art, New York 1954, p.203 f.

155 *Potlatch* (Zentralorgan der Lettristen), Number 14, November 1954. Quoted from *Spur 5*, Munich n.d., p.3.

156 *Baukunst und Werkform*, 10th year, Darmstadt 1957, Number 1. See also *Konrad Wachsmann, Wendepunkt im Bauen*, Krausskopf Verlag, Wiesbaden 1959, p.208.

157 First published by Reinhard Kaufman as *Schrift der Galerie Renate Boukes*, Wiesbaden 1958.

161 *Internationale Situationniste*, Paris 1963, Number 2.

163 Quoted from *Quadrat Blatt*, de Jong & Co., Hilversum 1961.

165 *Der Monat*, Berlin 1963, Number 174 (March), p.96.

167 Duplicated text. Compare the shortened version in *Mobile Architektur*, exhibition catalogue from the Galerie Seide, Hanover 1961.

169 *Zodiac*, Number 8, Milan, June 1961, p.20.

171 *Zero*, Vol. 3, Düsseldorf, n.d. (To be published in English by MIT Press, Cambridge, Massachusetts 1971, see p.130 f.)

172 *Internationale Situationniste*, Number 4, Paris, June 1960, p.36 ff.

175 Duplicated text.

177 Quoted from *Constant—Amsterdam*, exhibition catalogue of the Städt. Kunstgalerie Bochum, March/April 1961.

179 *Architectural Design*, London, August 1961.

181 Catalogue of the Hollein-Pichler exhibition, Vienna 1963.

183 Lecture, Essen, June 1962.

185 *Heimat – Deine Häuser!*, exhibition catalogue from the Landesgewerbeamt, Stuttgart 1963.

Index